THE FUTURE NOTARY

The Future Notary

Mastering RON, eNotary, and Complex Scenarios

DERRICK SPRUILL

Book edited by Lee Lee Trotter

Cover design, interior photos, and illustrations by Montes Travis

ISBN: 978-1-965-896-29-7

DEDICATION

This book is dedicated to the bold spirit of innovation, the unwavering pursuit of excellence, and the profound human connection that endures even as our world transforms.

To my beloved **wife**, whose constant encouragement and forward-looking perspective inspire me to embrace every new challenge, and to my **parents**, who instilled in me the foundational values of diligence and integrity—principles that are the timeless compass navigating the ever-evolving landscape of our profession.

And with a joyful heart, I dedicate this work to every Notary Public who dares to look beyond the horizon, to master new technologies, and to serve with compassion in the most complex and sensitive scenarios. May this guide empower you to embrace the digital future with confidence, to uphold the dignity of every signer, and to lead our noble profession into an era of unparalleled service, security, and boundless opportunity, all illuminated by the grace of our Lord and Savior Jesus Christ. May your vision be clear, and your impact be everlasting.

Legal Disclaimer:

The information provided in this book is for general informational and educational purposes only and is not intended to be a substitute for professional legal advice. While the author has made every effort to ensure the accuracy of the information, this book does not provide legal advice. Reading this book does not create an attorney-client relationship between the author and the reader. You should not act or refrain from acting based on any content included in this book without seeking legal or other professional advice. Readers are encouraged to consult with a qualified attorney licensed in their jurisdiction for advice specific to their individual circumstances. The author assumes no responsibility for errors or omissions, or for any damages that may result from the use of the information contained herein.

Table of Contents

Chapter 1: The Notary in the Digital Age: Adapting to the Future of Notarization 11

I. Introduction: Embracing the Digital Frontier – My Vision for Your Future 12

II. The Digital Notary Revolution: Why Now? 13

III. The Foundational Principles That Endure 14

IV. What the Modern Notary Must Master 15

Conclusion 16

Chapter 2: The Notary's New Frontier: Remote Online Notarization (RON) 17

I. Introduction: RON's Monumental Impact on the Notary Profession 18

II. The Legal and Technological Framework of RON 18

III. The Notary's Role in a RON Session 20

IV. Notary's Best Practices and RON Pitfalls to Avoid 21

V. The Future of Notarization: RON's Growing and Central Role 22

Chapter 3: Evolving with Technology: Electronic Notarization (eNotary) 24

I. Introduction: The eNotary as a Bridge Between Paper and Digital 25

II. The eNotary Process: The Digital In-Person Notarization 25

III. Becoming an eNotary: Requirements and Process 27

IV. Benefits and Challenges of Incorporating eNotary 28

V. eNotary's Place in the Modern Notary Landscape 29

Conclusion 29

Chapter 4: Special Considerations: Notarizing for Individuals with Disabilities 31

I. Introduction: Accessibility and Dignity in Notarization 31

II. Notarizing for Visually Impaired or Blind Signers 33

III. Notarizing for Signers with Physical Disabilities 35

IV. Notarizing for Signers with Communication Disabilities 36

V. The Notary's Guiding Principle: Protecting Autonomy 38

Conclusion 38

Chapter 5: Navigating High-Risk Environments: Hospitals, Jails, and Foreign Languages 40

I. Introduction: The Notary's Role in a High-Stakes World 41

II. Notarizing in Hospitals, Nursing Homes, and Assisted Living Facilities 42

III. Notarizing for Incarcerated Individuals 45

IV. Notarizing Documents in Foreign Languages 47

V. The Notary's Guiding Principle: Protecting Autonomy and "When in Doubt, Don't" 49

Conclusion 51

Chapter 6: The Notary as a Leader: Vision, Ethics, and The Next Generation 52

I. Introduction: The Legacy You Build 53

II. The Notary as a Professional and Entrepreneur 54

III. The Notary as an Ethical Compass 55

IV. The World of Little Notary Derrick: Inspiring the Next Generation 57

V. Conclusion 58

Chapter 7: The Notary Knowledge Series: A Lifelong Commitment to Excellence 59

I. Introduction: Celebrating Our Journey Together – The Full Notary Knowledge Series 60
II. The Pillars of Your Notary Knowledge: A Series Recap....61
III. Key Takeaways for Your Lifelong Journey 64
IV. Essential Next Steps & Follow-Up Information....66
V. A Final, Heartfelt Message of Empowerment....67
Bonus Chapter: Your Digital Compass: Finding RON & eNotary Laws and Providers by State....69
I. The Power of Proactive Research: Why Knowing Where to Look Matters....70
II. State-by-State Guide: Finding RON & eNotary Laws and Approved Providers Online (50 States + DC) 71
III. Conclusion: Your Personal Legal Navigation Tool for the Digital Age....85
Glossary of Key Terms....87
About the Author: Derrick Spruill....109
Derrick Spruill's Core Values 111
Derrick Spruill's Goals....111
Books by Derrick Spruill....112
End Notes for The Future Notary 113

Chapter 1: The Notary in the Digital Age: Adapting to the Future of Notarization

Hello, and welcome, my fellow Notary Knowledge seeker! It's me, Derrick Spruill, and I can't even begin to tell you how excited I am to be here with you for our final book in this incredible series, **"The Notary Future: Mastering RON, eNotary, and Complex Scenarios."** We've covered so much ground together, from the very foundations of the notary office to building a thriving mobile notary business. Now, it's time to put on our futuristic glasses and look ahead! The notary profession is dynamic, it's thrilling, and it is evolving at an electrifying pace. And I am absolutely thrilled to be a notary in this incredible moment, and I look forward with boundless energy and optimism to the future of notarization—a future that you and I will help shape.

I. Introduction: Embracing the Digital Frontier – My Vision for Your Future

When I first started Mobile Notary by Derrick Spruill, I was an absolute sponge for knowledge. I devoured everything I could about notary law, business strategy, and client service. And as I served my community in Herndon, Virginia, a new revolution was happening right under our noses: the digital transformation of our profession. It was a thrilling discovery! The world of notarization was no longer confined to paper and ink; it was expanding into the digital realm, offering new opportunities for convenience, security, and global reach. I felt an exhilarating sense of purpose, knowing that this was a chance not just to adapt, but to lead.

My Personal Journey from Paper to Digital: My journey from a notary who meticulously applied ink stamps to one who now uses an electronic seal on a digital document was born out of a desire for continuous improvement. I had always aimed for operational excellence (a topic we explored in-depth in *Notary Operational Excellence*), and technology presented a new frontier for that. I remember getting certified for Remote Online Notarization (RON) and being absolutely amazed by the technology. The first time I notarized a document for a client who was in another state, I felt like I was part of something monumental. The ease, the security, the sheer magic of it all was a revelation! It was a moment that reminded me that my passion for serving others had found a powerful new medium. It was a total game-changer.

Why Technology is Not a Threat, but an Opportunity: For some, new technology might seem daunting, a threat to the traditions of our profession. But I see it differently. I see it as a monumental opportunity! It's a chance to enhance our service, expand our reach, and provide a level of security that paper-based transactions simply can't match. As I often share on my "Notary Knowledge by Derrick Spruill" podcast, technology doesn't replace the notary; it elevates the notary! It frees us from the constraints of geography and paper, allowing us to focus on what truly matters: verifying identity, assessing willingness, and upholding the public trust. It's an inspiring new tool in our toolbox, not a replacement for us.

The Purpose of This Book: Your Blueprint for the Future: This book is your blueprint for this exciting new era. It's a guide to help you navigate the digital landscape with the same confidence and passion that you bring to your in-person signings. We'll demystify Remote Online Notarization (RON), clarify the nuances of Electronic Notarization (eNotary), and provide you with the tools to handle even the most complex and unusual scenarios with unwavering grace. By the end of this book, you'll not only be ready for the future of notarization—you'll be leading the charge!

II. The Digital Notary Revolution: Why Now?

The digital notary revolution isn't just a hypothetical concept; it's here, and it's happening all around us. There are compelling reasons for this rapid shift, and understanding them will help you position your business for success.

The Demand for Convenience and Speed: As a mobile notary, you've already experienced the power of convenience firsthand. Clients are busy, and they'll pay for a service that saves them time and effort. RON and eNotary take that convenience to the next level by eliminating travel entirely. This is a game-changer for clients who are homebound, geographically distant, or simply prefer a paperless, instantaneous transaction.

Global Reach and Remote Workforces: In our modern world, business and personal lives are no longer confined to a single location. Companies hire employees across the country (and the world), families move overseas, and international transactions are a daily reality. RON allows you to serve a global clientele, connecting your local expertise to a worldwide market. Imagine notarizing a power of attorney for a U.S. citizen working in Europe or a business contract for a company with partners in Asia—all from the comfort of your home office!

Enhanced Security and Fraud Prevention: This is one of the most compelling arguments for the digital notary revolution. While our meticulous practices in traditional notarization are vital, digital notarization offers layers of security that are incredibly difficult to bypass. The multi-layered identity verification process (credential analysis, knowledge-based authentication, and audio-visual recording) and the cryptographic security of the electronic seal create an incredibly robust fraud shield. A digital document is also tamper-evident; any change after the notarization is immediately detectable, a feature that physical paper can't match. This enhanced security is a massive win for everyone.

Business Continuity and Market Resilience: The digital revolution has also proven its value in times of crisis. During the recent pandemic, when in-person notarizations became challenging or impossible, RON provided a vital lifeline for individuals and businesses. It ensured that critical transactions—like real estate closings, wills, and medical directives—could still be completed safely and legally. Embracing RON ensures your business is resilient and can continue to operate and serve clients, even in the face of unforeseen disruptions. It's a fantastic form of business insurance!

III. The Foundational Principles That Endure

While the tools and technology of our profession are changing, the core principles that make the notary's office so important remain absolutely immutable. These are the timeless values that you, a Notary Public, must always embody, regardless of whether you're using an ink stamp or an electronic seal.

Impartiality: The Unchanging Cornerstone: Whether you're face-to-face or screen-to-screen, your role as an impartial witness is the unchanging cornerstone of your credibility. You must have no personal, financial, or familial interest in the transaction. Your ethical obligation to be a neutral third party remains paramount, ensuring trust in every notarization you perform.

The Oath of Office and Public Trust: When you took your oath of office, you made a solemn promise to serve the public with integrity. That promise doesn't change just because the notarization moves online. In fact, in the digital age, where trust can be more difficult to establish, your commitment to your oath and the public trust is more important than ever. You are a guardian of integrity, and that mission is timeless.

The Ministerial Role: Your Boundary Remains: This is a critical point that I often stress. Your role is, and will always be, ministerial. Technology does not give you a law degree! You cannot give legal advice, interpret documents, or choose the type of notarial act for a signer, whether you're using a pen or a digital certificate. Your boundary is your most powerful tool for your protection and for the protection of the public.

IV. What the Modern Notary Must Master

So, what does it take to succeed as a notary in this exciting new era? It requires a blend of traditional skills and new competencies. It's about being a lifelong learner who embraces change with an open mind and a joyful spirit.

Technology: Understanding the Tools of the Trade: You must be proficient in the new technologies that are shaping our profession. This includes mastering Remote Online Notarization (RON) platforms, electronic notarization (eNotary) software, and cybersecurity best practices. Don't be afraid of the learning curve; it's a new adventure, and every new skill you acquire expands your potential.

Compliance: Navigating New and Complex Laws: The legal landscape for digital notarization is complex and state-specific. You must be diligent in understanding and complying with the laws of your commissioning state regarding RON and eNotary. This includes knowing the requirements for identity verification, electronic journaling, and document acceptance.

Vigilance: Detecting New Forms of Fraud: Just as fraudsters adapted to paper-based notarization, they are also attempting to exploit new technologies. You must be vigilant in detecting new forms of digital fraud, such as sophisticated fake IDs that bypass security checks or attempts to manipulate a virtual signing environment. Your human judgment remains your ultimate defense.

Professionalism: Maintaining Excellence in Any Environment: Whether you're in a client's living room or on a video call, your professionalism is paramount. Be punctual (log in on time!), prepared (have your technology working!), and courteous. Your demeanor, communication, and attention to detail must be impeccable in any environment.

Conclusion

The future of notarization is not a distant, mysterious place; it's a dynamic, exciting, and empowering reality that you are stepping into right now. My journey has taught me that the core principles of our profession are timeless, but our tools and methods must evolve to meet the needs of a modern world. By embracing new technologies like RON and eNotary with enthusiasm, committing to a proactive mindset of continuous learning, and upholding your foundational values of integrity and public trust, you will not only be ready for the future—you'll be a leader within it. So, let's step confidently into this new era, equipped, inspired, and excited for the journey ahead. The future of notarization is bright, and you are a vital part of it!

Chapter 2: The Notary's New Frontier: Remote Online Notarization (RON)

The digital revolution has ushered in a groundbreaking new era for the notary profession, one that is reshaping how we serve our clients and uphold the public trust. At the forefront of this transformation is **Remote Online Notarization (RON)**, a technology that has redefined the very concept of "personal appearance" by allowing notarial acts to be performed entirely virtually, transcending geographical boundaries. RON is a monumental leap forward, and for any notary committed to excellence and future-proofing their practice, mastering it is no longer an option—it is a powerful opportunity.

I. Introduction: RON's Monumental Impact on the Notary Profession

For generations, traditional notarization has steadfastly required the physical, in-person presence of the signer before the notary. This was a cornerstone principle designed to ensure identity verification and voluntary consent. RON challenges this tradition by replicating these essential elements in a secure digital environment. It allows a notary and a signer to complete a notarization when they are in different physical locations, communicating seamlessly via a secure, real-time audio-visual link over the internet.

What RON Is and How It Differs from Traditional Notarization: RON is a legally valid notarial act performed by a commissioned notary public where the signer is **not** in the physical presence of the notary. The document being notarized is an electronic document (e.g., a PDF file), the signer affixes an electronic signature (e-signature), and the notary applies an electronic notary seal and an electronic notary signature.

The core difference is the method of personal appearance. For traditional notarization, the signer must be physically in the same room as the notary. For RON, the notary and signer are physically separate, but connected through a state-approved, secure audio-visual technology. This virtual interaction simulates the in-person experience as closely as possible, allowing for real-time observation and communication.

II. The Legal and Technological Framework of RON

RON is far more than just a video call or a simple electronic signature. It is a highly regulated and technologically sophisticated process built upon a foundation of advanced digital tools and stringent security measures meticulously designed to ensure the integrity, authenticity, and legal validity of the notarial act in a virtual environment.

State-Specific Authorization: Your Commission for the Digital World: The adoption of RON is governed by state law. To perform RON notarizations, a notary must:

- First, be a currently commissioned traditional notary public in a state that permits RON.
- Second, receive a specific authorization or endorsement from their state's commissioning authority to act as a RON notary. This often requires completing a mandatory training course and sometimes an exam.
- Third, register with the state as a RON notary.

This additional authorization ensures that notaries who perform RON acts have the necessary specialized knowledge of the technology, security protocols, and state-specific legal requirements.

The Approved RON Platform: Your Virtual Office: Notaries are legally mandated to use a RON platform that has been specifically approved by their commissioning state's regulatory authority. These are not generic video conferencing tools like Zoom or FaceTime. State approval ensures the platform meets rigorous security, identity verification, and record-keeping standards. Approved RON platforms provide a comprehensive, integrated environment for the entire notarization process, including:

- **Secure Audio-Visual Technology:** High-quality, encrypted video and audio feeds that allow for clear, real-time interaction between the notary and signer, simulating the in-person experience. The notary must be able to see and hear the signer clearly.
- **Electronic Journal (e-journal):** An integrated, tamper-evident digital journal that automatically records details of the notarization, including the date, time, and identity verification methods used.
- **Electronic Notary Seal and Signature:** Secure mechanisms for the notary to apply their unique electronic seal and signature to the digital document. These are cryptographically secured using digital certificates.

- **Mandatory Audio-Visual Recording and Storage:** The platform is responsible for recording and securely storing the entire RON session for a legally mandated retention period. This recording is a critical audit trail.

III. The Notary's Role in a RON Session

While the environment is virtual, the notary's core duties and responsibilities remain the same, but with enhanced procedural steps. The notary is still a human firewall.

The Multi-Layered Identity Verification Process (Enhanced Security): RON identity verification is often significantly more rigorous and technologically advanced than traditional methods, providing a robust defense against impersonation. The notary must ensure the signer's identity through a combination of:

- **Credential Analysis of Signer's ID:** This technology automatically scans the signer's government-issued ID (e.g., driver's license, passport) for security features (such as holograms and micro-printing) and compares them against forensic databases of known ID templates. This helps detect sophisticated forgeries.
- **Knowledge-Based Authentication (KBA):** The signer answers a series of challenging personal questions (e.g., "Which of these addresses have you lived at?") generated from public and private data sources. These questions are designed to be difficult for anyone but the true individual to answer correctly.
- **Visual and Audio Confirmation:** During the live video conference, the notary visually and audibly confirms the signer's identity, comparing their appearance to their ID and observing their responses to KBA questions. This is where the notary's human judgment and observational skills are paramount.

Conducting the Notarization (A Step-by-Step Guide): Once identity is verified, the notary proceeds with the notarization in a virtual environment:

1. **Confirm Awareness and Willingness:** The notary assesses that the signer is appearing willingly and understands the nature of the document. This is done through live verbal communication and observation of the signer's demeanor.
2. **Verbal Oath or Acknowledgment:** The notary administers a verbal oath or receives a verbal acknowledgment from the signer, just as in an in-person notarization.
3. **Manage the E-signing and E-sealing Process:** The notary guides the signer to apply their electronic signature to the document within the platform. The notary then applies their own electronic signature and seal. These electronic marks are cryptographically sealed to the document, making it tamper-evident.
4. **The Critical Audit Trail:** The notary's actions, along with the audio-visual recording of the entire session, are automatically logged in the e-journal, creating a comprehensive and irrefutable record of the notarial act.

IV. Notary's Best Practices and RON Pitfalls to Avoid

While RON is powerful, it is not without its pitfalls. A diligent notary must be aware of best practices to ensure compliance and avoid common errors.

Ensuring Document Acceptance with Receiving Parties:

- **Not all jurisdictions are created equal.** While a notarization may be legally valid in the commissioning state, the receiving party (e.g., a county recorder's office in a state that does not accept RON, or a foreign government) may not be equipped or legally authorized to accept the electronic document.
- **Best Practice:** Always confirm with the receiving party (e.g., the title company, lender, or legal firm) that they will accept a

RON-notarized document *before* the session. This proactive step saves time and prevents frustration.

Adhering to UPL Prohibitions in a Virtual Environment:

- The prohibition against the Unauthorized Practice of Law (UPL) is just as strict in a virtual environment as it is in person. Notaries must never give legal advice, interpret documents, or choose a notarial act for the signer.
- **Best Practice:** Use a clear "no legal advice" script and be prepared to confidently refer signers to a licensed attorney, even over a video call.

Handling Technological Glitches and Connectivity Issues:

- A stable internet connection is essential. If the video or audio quality is poor, or if the connection is lost during the session, the notary **must** stop the notarization and either reconnect or reschedule. The notary must be able to clearly see and hear the signer for the entire session.
- **Best Practice:** Have a backup internet connection (e.g., a mobile hotspot). Test your equipment and connection before each session.

Strict Compliance with Signer Location Rules:

- While RON allows the signer to be in a different location, a notary must know their state's specific rules regarding where the signer can be located. Some states allow international signers, while others restrict the signer to a U.S. state.
- **Best Practice:** Verify the signer's physical location at the beginning of every RON session and ensure it complies with your state's laws.

V. The Future of Notarization: RON's Growing and Central Role

Remote Online Notarization is not merely a passing trend; it is rapidly becoming a standard and increasingly central offering in the notary profession. Driven by an insatiable demand for convenience, the inherent security advantages of digital processes, and continuous technological advancements, its adoption has accelerated significantly. Notaries who proactively embrace RON, invest in the necessary training and technology, and diligently adhere to its specific legal and security protocols are positioning themselves not just for short-term gains, but for long-term relevance, resilience, and sustained success in a rapidly digitizing world. The future of notarization is undeniably digital, and a knowledgeable, prepared notary is at its forefront.

Chapter 3: Evolving with Technology: Electronic Notarization (eNotary)

Hey there, future-focused notary! It's Derrick Spruill, and I'm so excited to dive into another crucial topic that's defining our future. We've talked about embracing the digital age and unlocking a new frontier with Remote Online Notarization (RON). Now, get ready for another crucial player on the field that deserves our enthusiastic attention: **Electronic Notarization, or eNotary!** This isn't just a stepping stone; it's a brilliant, powerful tool that bridges the gap between our traditional paper-based practices and the cutting-edge, fully digital future. Mastering eNotary is a fantastic way to streamline your in-person services, boost efficiency, and show your clients that you are a notary who is ready for anything the modern age throws your way. Let's power up our in-person notarial acts and add some digital magic!

I. Introduction: The eNotary as a Bridge Between Paper and Digital

Imagine this: You've arrived at an appointment, and the client, with a big smile, pulls out a tablet with a digital document, ready to go completely paperless. Do you have to say, "Sorry, I only work with paper?" Absolutely not! With eNotary, you can respond with a cheerful and confident, "Yes, I'm ready for that!" The client's relief will be palpable. ENotary is the notarization act performed on an electronic document, but with a key and wonderful difference from RON: the signer is right there in your **physical presence**. You're both in the same room, but instead of using a traditional ink pad, the document and all your notary tools are digital.

This isn't just about saving paper; it’s about making your in-person notarizations faster, more secure, and perfectly integrated into the digital world. Think of it as a logical and exciting upgrade to your traditional services, allowing you to meet a growing demand for paperless, efficient workflows with a sense of fun. It's a fantastic way to expand your service offerings and build an even more modern, professional reputation.

II. The eNotary Process: The Digital In-Person Notarization

The eNotary process is where you take all your meticulous, trustworthy in-person skills and apply them to a digital environment. It’s truly the best of both worlds! You get all the comfort and personal connection of a face-to-face meeting, combined with the security and efficiency of digital technology.

The Notary's Role and Responsibilities: Your Digital Superpowers Your role as an eNotary is still that of a guardian of trust, but with a digital toolkit. You:

- **Verify Identity:** You still perform a rigorous, in-person ID check, but now you have a new superpower! You're also using the technology to capture and record the ID data digitally. It's a win-win for security and record-keeping that makes your job even more robust!
- **Assess Awareness and Willingness:** Your human judgment and keen observation skills are still paramount. You're looking the signer right in the eye, listening to their voice, and ensuring with absolute certainty that they are signing voluntarily and with understanding. No technology can replace your crucial human touch.
- **Guide the Digital Signing:** You guide the signer to apply their electronic signature to the electronic document using a signature pad or a tablet. It's a fun, modern moment that delights clients who are tired of looking for a pen!
- **Apply Your Digital Marks:** This is where the magic truly happens! You apply your electronic notary seal and your electronic signature, which are not just digital pictures. They are cryptographically secured to the document, making it instantly tamper-evident.
- **Maintain the E-Journal:** You maintain a secure electronic journal (e-journal) where all the details of the notarization are automatically and meticulously recorded. Say goodbye to messy handwriting and hello to a flawless, digital record!

The Signer's Experience: E-signatures and Digital Documents: For the signer, the process is streamlined, modern, and often a pleasant surprise! They get to:

- **Sign Digitally:** They use an e-signature to sign the document on a tablet, a computer, or a signature pad. It's quick, clean, and futuristic!
- **Receive Instantly:** Once the notarization is complete, they can receive the tamper-evident, notarized electronic document

instantly via email. This is an immediate, paperless, and incredibly convenient final product that saves them the hassle of scanning or filing.

- **Enhanced Security:** They get the peace of mind of a document that is cryptographically sealed, meaning any change to the document after your e-seal is applied will be immediately detectable. They know their document is a digital fortress.

Security and Tamper-Evidence: The Notary's Digital Magic This is truly the magic of eNotary! Your electronic seal and signature aren't just a picture; they are a sophisticated digital credential. When you apply your digital seal, it creates a cryptographic "digital fingerprint" of the entire electronic document. This fingerprint is then encrypted with your private key and embedded into the document. If any part of that electronic document is altered or tampered with *after* you've applied your signature, the digital fingerprint will change, and your electronic seal will show as invalid. This provides an incredibly robust, tamper-evident audit trail that physical paper often cannot match. It's notary magic in action!

III. Becoming an eNotary: Requirements and Process

Becoming an eNotary is a clear and exciting path to modernization. The specific requirements vary by state, but the process is designed to be a seamless extension of your traditional commission.

State-Specific Registration and Commissioning:

- You must first be a commissioned traditional notary in a state that permits eNotary. This is your foundational notarial superpower.
- You will then need to apply and register specifically as an eNotary with your state's commissioning authority (e.g., the Secretary of State's office). This ensures you have the official authorization to perform these digital acts.

Approved eNotary Software and Digital Certificates:

- You are legally required to use eNotary software or a platform that has been specifically approved by your commissioning state. These platforms provide all the tools you need for the digital signing ceremony.
- You will also need to obtain a digital certificate, a unique electronic credential that links your electronic signature and seal to your identity as a notary. This is often provided through your approved technology provider and is a one-time setup that unlocks your digital notary powers!

IV. Benefits and Challenges of Incorporating eNotary

Embracing eNotary is a fantastic way to modernize your practice and show your clients you're ready for the future.

Benefits for Notaries: Leveling Up Your Practice

- **Increased Efficiency and Green Practice:** Say goodbye to the paper mess, the ink smudges, and the tedious scanning! ENotary streamlines your in-person workflow, reduces printing and scanning costs, and is an environmentally friendly practice that clients love. It's all about making your business smarter and more sustainable!
- **Enhanced Security:** The cryptographic security and tamper-evident nature of eNotary documents provide a more robust audit trail and a powerful defense against fraud. You get the peace of mind of knowing your digital documents are protected by a digital fortress.
- **Modernization and Competitive Edge:** By offering eNotary, you appeal to tech-savvy clients and businesses that prioritize digital workflows. It provides a unique and modern competitive advantage, showing you're a notary who is ready for the future, not stuck in the past. It's a great conversation starter and brand builder!

Challenges for Notaries: Leveling Up Your Skills

- **Technology Dependence:** A minor hiccup with your software, tablet, or a poor internet connection could disrupt a signing. It's important to be prepared for technology! This means having a backup plan (like a fully charged tablet or a paper alternative ready to go), and a positive attitude to navigate any glitches with grace and a smile.
- **Upfront Investment:** There may be costs associated with software subscriptions and a digital certificate. But think of it as an exciting investment in your future-proofed business, a small cost for a big payoff in efficiency and professionalism.
- **Signer Familiarity:** Some clients may be unfamiliar with e-signatures or digital documents. But that's where you shine! You get to be the helpful, patient, and knowledgeable guide who walks them through the process with a smile. You'll make them feel comfortable and confident, turning a new experience into a great one.

V. eNotary's Place in the Modern Notary Landscape

Electronic notarization (eNotary), while distinct from RON, is an integral and vital part of the advanced notary landscape. It's a bridge that allows notaries to embrace digital workflows for in-person transactions, enhancing efficiency and security without losing the personal connection of a face-to-face meeting. By proactively becoming an eNotary, you are not just keeping up with technology; you are paving the way for a more efficient, secure, and modern notary experience for everyone. It's a fantastic addition to your notary practice, complementing both traditional and remote offerings and ensuring you're ready for whatever the future holds! It's a lively, fun, and exciting time to be a notary, and eNotary is a key part of that adventure.

Conclusion

As we power down this chapter, I want you to feel the electrifying excitement of eNotary! This is a fantastic new tool that takes everything you've already mastered—your in-person skills, your meticulous attention to detail, and your commitment to integrity—and supercharges it for the digital age. It's an opportunity to serve clients in a more modern, secure, and efficient way, while still enjoying the personal connection of a face-to-face meeting. So, get ready to embrace the digital future, learn the new skills, and add eNotary to your impressive toolkit. The future of notarization is bright, it's exciting, and it's waiting for you to lead the way!

Chapter 4: Special Considerations: Notarizing for Individuals with Disabilities

Hello again, my fellow Notary Public, and welcome to a chapter that is close to my heart. It's me, Derrick Spruill, and I'm thrilled to guide you through what I consider to be some of the most sensitive and rewarding aspects of our profession. We've talked about the notary's new digital frontier, but now let's ground ourselves in the human element. The notary's service, at its core, is about **accessibility and dignity**. It's about being a guardian of trust for *everyone*, and that includes individuals who may have physical, visual, or communication disabilities. This chapter is a sensitive and practical guide to navigating these situations, ensuring their rights are protected and the notarization is performed compliantly and with the utmost respect.

I. Introduction: Accessibility and Dignity in Notarization

My journey as a mobile notary has taken me all over Northern Virginia, from bustling business parks to quiet residential homes. I've been to hospitals and rehabilitation centers, and I've seen firsthand how crucial our service is to those with limited mobility. It's a humbling and inspiring experience. I recall a time I was called to a nursing home to notarize a Power of Attorney for an elderly woman. She was a bit frail, but her mind was as sharp as a tack. She had a wonderful sense of humor and was so grateful that I came to her, saying it saved her a stressful trip and made a difficult process feel so much easier. That day, I realized that my service wasn't just a business; it was a way to provide dignity and a sense of normalcy in a challenging time. It's in these moments that the human connection, built on respect and care, truly elevates the notarial act.

The Notary's Ethical Obligation to Accommodate: Our commission is a public trust, and with that comes an ethical obligation to accommodate signers with disabilities. This isn't just a matter of politeness; it's about ensuring **equal access to a vital public service**. The law requires us to be impartial to all signers, and that means we must make reasonable accommodations to ensure that all parties have the opportunity to execute their documents compliantly. This commitment to accessibility is a huge part of what makes being a notary so inspiring. It's about empowering people, ensuring their voice is heard, and their legal rights are protected, regardless of their physical or cognitive circumstances. This is a core value that should guide every decision you make when serving this community.

My Personal Experience Serving Clients with Disabilities: I've had the honor of notarizing for a visually impaired man who, with a trusted loved one reading the document to him, was able to confirm his wishes and sign with confidence. The sense of trust in that room was palpable, and my role was to facilitate his autonomy. I've also helped a man in a wheelchair who was unable to travel, and we completed his signing right in his living room, with my clipboard serving as a flat, stable signing surface. Each of these experiences was a powerful reminder of our profession's profound human impact. It’s not just about the document; it's about the dignity and care we show to every individual we serve, making a stressful or difficult process feel seamless and respectful.

II. Notarizing for Visually Impaired or Blind Signers

Accommodating signers who are blind or visually impaired requires a delicate balance of careful procedure and respectful communication. Your goal is to ensure they can, with appropriate and legally permissible assistance, satisfy the core requirements of the notarial act, especially the assessment of awareness and willingness. This is where your trust and integrity become their eyes.

Ensuring Awareness: Document Review and Verbal Confirmation:

- **The Challenge:** A signer who is blind or visually impaired cannot visually review the document. This means you cannot simply assume they understand its contents or that there are no blank spaces that could be fraudulently filled in later. It is a critical risk you must address.
- **Best Practices:** You must ensure the signer has had the opportunity to review and fully understand the document's contents. You should never, under any circumstances, read the document to the signer yourself unless you are a licensed attorney. However, you can and should:
    - **Confirm Prior Review:** Begin the process by asking the signer if they have already had the document read to them by a trusted individual (e.g., their attorney, family member, or friend), and if they feel they fully understand its contents. This initial check establishes their prior knowledge.
    - **Allow a Trusted Reader:** The signer can have a trusted person (not a party to the document or a beneficiary) read the document aloud to them in your presence. As the notary, you should be present to observe the process, and you should then verbally confirm with the signer that they heard and understood

what was read. This ensures transparency and gives you an opportunity to assess their lucidity.

- **State Document Type Aloud:** You should always clearly state the title and type of the document aloud to the signer (e.g., "I'm holding a Power of Attorney"). This is your way of confirming the nature of the document for your record and for their benefit, ensuring they know what document is being signed.
- **Verbal Confirmation of Willingness:** You must verbally confirm with the signer that they are signing the document voluntarily and that it represents their true wishes. Ask, "Are you signing this document of your own free will?" and "Does this document represent your wishes?" The verbal response is a crucial part of the process.

Executing the Signature: Guiding the Hand vs. Signature by Mark:

- **The Challenge:** The signer may be unable to see the signature line to sign their name or may be unable to write a legible signature due to their visual impairment.
- **Best Practices:** Your role is to assist with the physical act of signing without compromising the intent of the signer. You must assist without leading or controlling the outcome.
    - **Guiding the Hand:** You, or a trusted third party, may physically guide the signer's hand to the correct signature line, but only **if expressly requested by the signer** and **only to position the hand**. You cannot assist in the actual formation of the signature itself. The signer must maintain physical control over the pen during the signing.
    - **Signature by Mark:** If the signer cannot write their name, they may make a "signature by mark" (e.g., an "X" or other distinct symbol). Your state's laws will dictate the precise procedure for this. Typically, this requires **two disinterested witnesses** to be present who sign next to the mark and attest that it is the

signer's mark. You then notarize the mark, documenting the process meticulously in your journal. You **cannot** be one of these witnesses, as it would compromise your impartiality.

- **Journal Entry and Documentation:** Your notary journal entry must be exceptionally thorough. Note that the signer is visually impaired, how their identity was verified, and if a third party assisted with their hand or if a signature by mark was used. This meticulous record is your key defense in case of a later dispute, as it demonstrates that you took all appropriate measures to ensure compliance.

III. Notarizing for Signers with Physical Disabilities

Accommodating signers with physical limitations requires patience, flexibility, and a focus on ensuring the signing environment is accessible and conducive to a proper notarial act. Your empathy and problem-solving skills shine brightly here.

Making Accommodations: Mobility, Location, and Signing Surface:

- **The Challenge:** Signers may be unable to travel to a notary, move easily within a location, or have difficulty holding a pen.
- **Best Practices:** This is where being a mobile notary is an absolute superpower! Your service, by its very nature, is a powerful accommodation.
    - **Choose an Accessible Location:** You are a mobile notary! Your willingness to travel to a home, hospital, or care facility is the primary and most significant accommodation you can offer. This removes the major barrier of mobility.
    - **Suitable Environment:** When you arrive, politely ask for an accessible, well-lit area with a stable surface. I always carry a rigid clipboard in my notary bag for this exact reason. This allows a signer in bed or in a wheelchair to have a firm, flat surface to sign on

without compromising the quality of the notarization. A signing surface on a lap or an unstable surface is a risk to document integrity.

  - **Maintain Professionalism:** Your tone should be encouraging and uplifting. Do not make assumptions about their abilities. Treat the client with the same professionalism and respect you would for any other signing, focusing on their autonomy and dignity.

Assisting with the Signature (When Necessary and Under Signer's Direction):

- **The Challenge:** The signer may have difficulty holding a pen or forming a legible signature due to a physical disability (e.g., arthritis, tremors, a stroke).
- **Best Practices:** Your role is to assist with the *physical act of signing* without compromising the *intent of the signer*. The signer's will is paramount.
  - **Signature Assistance:** The signer may direct another person (not a party to the document or a beneficiary) to assist them in holding the pen, but this must be done **under the signer's direct and clear physical control or explicit verbal instruction**. You must witness this, and the signer's intent must be unambiguous. You **cannot** assume the signer wants assistance; they must direct it.
  - **Signature by Mark:** If the signer cannot form a signature, they can use a "signature by mark" if your state permits, following the procedures for witnesses.
  - **Journal Entry:** Your journal is your shield here. Document in detail how the signer's signature was executed and any assistance provided. For example, "Signer's hand was guided by John Doe, as directed by the signer." This record proves your compliance.

IV. Notarizing for Signers with Communication Disabilities

Ensuring clear, direct, and effective communication is essential for the notary's duty to assess awareness and willingness. This can be challenging if the signer has a hearing, speech, or language impairment. Your ability to adapt and facilitate communication is key.

The Importance of Effective Communication:

- **The Challenge:** You must be able to communicate effectively with the signer to ask the necessary questions to assess their awareness and willingness. If there is a communication barrier that you cannot overcome, you cannot perform your duties properly.
- **Best Practices:**
  - **Effective Communication:** If the signer has a hearing impairment, communication can often be facilitated by writing notes or through sign language (if you or an interpreter are proficient). For a speech impairment, patience, active listening, and a calm, unhurried pace are paramount.
  - **Refusal:** If you cannot satisfy yourself that you can communicate effectively enough to assess the signer's awareness and willingness, you **must** refuse the notarization. Your inability to communicate directly is a legal barrier, as you cannot fulfill your duty to ensure the signer is aware of what they are doing.

Using Interpreters and Third-Party Assistance:

- **The Challenge:** A signer may not speak English, creating a language barrier.
- **Best Practices:**
  - **The Signer Must Understand:** Your notarization is about the *signer's* understanding, not yours. The signer must understand the document. You, as the notary, are not required to understand the document's content, but you must be able to communicate with the signer.
  - **Using an Interpreter:** Your state law will dictate if and how you can use an interpreter. The interpreter

must be impartial (not a party to the document or a beneficiary) and may need to provide a sworn statement (affidavit) attesting to the accuracy of their translation. The interpreter's role is to facilitate communication, not to provide legal advice or explain the document's content.

- **Journal Entry:** When using an interpreter, document their name, address, and how they were identified in your journal. Note that they acted as an interpreter for the signer.

V. The Notary's Guiding Principle: Protecting Autonomy

In all complex legal scenarios involving disabilities or impairments, your guiding principle must be to **protect the signer's autonomy and dignity** above all else. This means your role is to facilitate their wishes, not to question them, make assumptions about their abilities, or allow others to speak for them. Your vigilance ensures that the notarization reflects the true, unhindered will of the signer. It's not about making a difficult person sign; it's about making sure a vulnerable person has their will honored and their legal rights protected. This is the heart of compassionate service.

Conclusion

Navigating complex legal scenarios with disabilities is an honor and a privilege. It's a true test of your compassion, patience, and unwavering adherence to professional standards. By understanding how to accommodate signers with visual, physical, or communication disabilities, and by steadfastly refusing to compromise on your assessment of awareness and willingness, you fulfill your vital role as an indispensable guardian of trust. Your commitment to protecting the autonomy and dignity of every individual, regardless of their circumstances, is a testament to your professional integrity and a cornerstone of your service. So go forth, my fellow notary, with a compassionate heart and a meticulous mind, and continue to make a profound difference in the lives of those you serve.

Chapter 5: Navigating High-Risk Environments: Hospitals, Jails, and Foreign Languages

Hello again, my fellow Notary Public! It's me, Derrick Spruill, and I'm thrilled to be back with you for another exciting and impactful chapter of **"The Future Notary."** We've explored the thrilling digital frontiers of RON and eNotary, embracing technology with open arms. We've also grounded ourselves in the profound human dignity of serving those with disabilities, understanding that our service is truly for everyone. Now, let's talk about the moments when your notary skills, your composure, and your ethical compass are truly put to the ultimate test: **navigating high-risk environments**. These aren't your everyday kitchen table signings; these are the scenarios that demand a different level of preparedness, an extra dose of unwavering vigilance, and a huge, unwavering commitment to your ethical compass and personal safety. This chapter is a must-have guide for your notary toolkit, helping you confidently, safely, and joyfully notarize in places like hospitals, nursing homes, and jails, and for documents presented in foreign languages. Get ready to shine brightly in the most challenging situations!

I. Introduction: The Notary's Role in a High-Stakes World

My journey as a mobile notary has taken me all over Northern Virginia, from bustling business parks to quiet residential homes. I've been to hospitals and rehabilitation centers, and I've even found myself navigating the unique protocols of correctional facilities. Each of these environments, while requiring my consistent professionalism, demands a different kind of preparation and a heightened sense of awareness. The documents often carry immense personal or legal weight, and the circumstances surrounding the signing can be emotionally charged or fraught with potential for undue influence.

Why These Scenarios Require a Different Level of Preparedness: Think of a standard notary appointment as a calm, professional meeting, like a well-rehearsed play. Now, imagine a high-stakes notarization as an exciting, yet intensely live and unpredictable event. You need to be ready for anything and everything! In a hospital, you're not just notarizing; you're navigating a complex medical environment, the emotional stress of a patient's family, and potentially the patient's delicate health condition. In a jail, you're operating under strict security protocols with heightened risks of duress or even personal safety concerns. With a foreign language document, you're relying entirely on the signer's honesty and your own unwavering adherence to your legal boundaries, without understanding a single word yourself. These are precisely the moments where your foundational training (from *The Notary Public Foundation*), your operational excellence (from *Notary Operational Excellence*), and your fraud detection skills (from *Notary Fraud Shield*) truly pay off, and your vigilance becomes your ultimate superpower! It's about being a calm, steady presence in moments of potential chaos or vulnerability.

My Experiences in Hospitals and with International Documents: I'll never forget a time when I was called to a hospital late one night to notarize a document for a client in immense pain from a recent car accident. Amidst the flurry of nurses and doctors, the hushed urgency of the medical staff, and the palpable worry of his family, I had to find a quiet corner of the room, calmly verify his ID, and patiently assess his willingness and awareness. It was a stressful environment, but my commitment to my job—my professional mantra of "staying in the moment"—made sure I got it right. I focused solely on him, ensuring his autonomy was protected. That experience, which I often share on my "Notary Knowledge by Derrick Spruill" podcast, deeply reinforced the human impact of our work. I've also had the thrill of notarizing documents for international clients, and the joy of helping a client get an Apostille for their diploma to take to South Korea. The gratitude from clients navigating these complex, often life-changing, scenarios is incredibly inspiring. These are the moments that truly make this job so rewarding and why mastering these high-stakes environments is so important. It's about being a beacon of calm and competence when it matters most.

II. Notarizing in Hospitals, Nursing Homes, and Assisted Living Facilities

Notarizing for a client in a hospital, nursing home, or assisted living facility is a frequent, incredibly rewarding, and often time-sensitive service for a mobile notary. It requires a special blend of compassion, unwavering professionalism, and heightened vigilance, as these settings often present unique challenges to assessing a signer's true intent.

The Challenge: Assessing Willingness and Awareness in a Medical Setting:

- **The Challenge:** Signers in medical or care facilities may be elderly, seriously ill, recovering from surgery, or under the influence of strong medication (e.g., pain relievers, sedatives) that could significantly affect their mental capacity, lucidity, or ability to communicate clearly. They may also be under subtle or overt pressure from family members, caregivers, or other parties to sign documents (a potential for **undue influence** or coercion). Your primary duty is to assess their awareness and willingness to sign, and it's crucial to remember that you are **not a medical professional** and cannot diagnose mental competency. Your assessment is based on *apparent* understanding and free will.
- **Best Practices:**
    - **Observe and Engage Meticulously:** Look for clear signs of lucidity, coherence, and responsiveness. Is the signer oriented to time, place, and person? Are they making eye contact? Are they responding appropriately to their environment and to your initial greetings? Do they seem disoriented, unusually quiet, overly agitated, or lethargic? Are their responses delayed or inappropriate to the context of the conversation? Engage the signer directly with simple, non-leading questions (e.g., "Do you know what this document is about?", "Are you signing this voluntarily?", "Who is named in this document?"). Listen intently to their answers and observe their demeanor.
    - **Privacy First, Always:** If you have *any* doubt about the signer's free will or capacity due to the presence of third parties (e.g., a family member hovering, a caregiver speaking for them), politely but firmly ask any family or friends to step out of the room so you can speak privately with the signer. Explain that this is a legal requirement to ensure the notarization is valid and that the signer is acting of their own free

will. If they refuse to leave, it's a major red flag, and you **must** refuse the notarization. Document this refusal and the reason meticulously in your notary journal.

- **Heightened Vigilance for Red Flags:** Be extra vigilant for all red flags of duress, undue influence, or diminished capacity (as thoroughly discussed in *Notary Fraud Shield*). This includes observing body language, listening for whispered instructions, or noting any hesitation before signing. If you have concerns, it's always better to err on the side of caution and protect the vulnerable signer.

Working with Medical Staff and Family Members:

- **The Challenge:** You are a visitor in a medical environment, which has its own protocols and priorities. Medical staff and family members may be worried about the patient's well-being, or may inadvertently (or intentionally) try to influence the signing process.
- **Best Practices:**
    - **Professionalism and Respect:** Always be courteous and respectful of the medical staff's duties and the patient's privacy. Do not interrupt medical care or demand special privileges. Explain your presence calmly and professionally.
    - **Clear Communication of Your Role:** Clearly explain your role as an impartial notary. If you need to speak with the signer privately, explain that it's a legal requirement to ensure the notarization is valid and that you are assessing the signer's free will. Be firm but polite in setting these boundaries.
    - **Avoid Medical Advice:** Never engage in discussions about the patient's medical condition, prognosis, or treatment. Your role is strictly limited to the notarial act.

Privacy, Safety, and Journaling in a Public/Private Environment:

- **The Challenge:** Hospitals and care facilities are often semi-public spaces, but the documents and the signer's personal information are highly private and confidential. You must balance these factors while ensuring your own safety.
- **Best Practices:**
    - **Protect Private Information:** When making a journal entry, always shield the book from the view of others. Do not leave documents containing sensitive Personally Identifiable Information (PII) unattended or visible to unauthorized eyes. Use document folders or a secure bag (as discussed in *The Mobile Notary Blueprint*) to transport documents discreetly.
    - **Prioritize Safety:** If you feel unsafe in a hospital or care facility setting (e.g., due to an agitated family member, an unfamiliar wing, or a general sense of unease), politely excuse yourself and leave. Your personal safety is paramount and should never be compromised. Document the refusal in your journal and notify your commissioning authority if necessary.
    - **Document Everything Meticulously:** Your notary journal is your shield here. In addition to the standard entry, make detailed notes about the specific location within the facility (e.g., "Room 312, North Wing"), the signer's apparent demeanor, and any third parties present. If any concerns about willingness or awareness arose and were resolved (or led to a refusal), document those observations meticulously. This record is invaluable in case of a later dispute or legal challenge.

III. Notarizing for Incarcerated Individuals

Notarizing documents in jails, prisons, or correctional facilities is an incredibly important service, providing essential access to legal processes for incarcerated individuals. However, it presents unique logistical and safety challenges that require you to be a super-prepared, super-vigilant, and highly disciplined professional.

The Challenge: Security and Duress:

- **The Challenge:** You're entering a highly controlled, secure environment with strict security protocols. The signer (the inmate) may be under duress or pressure from other inmates, staff, or external parties. They may also lack a standard form of government-issued ID, relying on inmate identification. The potential for fraud or coercion is significantly heightened.
- **Best Practices:**
    - **Pre-Arrange with Facility (Non-Negotiable):** You **must** contact the correctional facility beforehand to understand and adhere to their specific rules for notaries. This includes their appointment scheduling procedures, acceptable ID for inmates (e.g., an inmate ID card issued by the facility is often acceptable, but always confirm), and all security protocols (e.g., what items you can bring in, escort requirements, designated signing areas). Never just show up unannounced.
    - **Follow All Rules Strictly:** Adhere strictly to every rule the facility sets forth, no matter how minor it seems. This is for your safety, the facility's security, and to ensure the notarization is not invalidated. Any deviation can lead to immediate termination of the visit.
    - **Assess Awareness/Willingness (Heightened Vigilance):** Pay **heightened attention** to signs of duress or confusion. Ensure the inmate is signing voluntarily and understands the document. Be particularly wary of other inmates or guards attempting to influence the signing or speaking for the inmate. If you suspect coercion, you **must** refuse.

  - **ID Verification (Facility-Specific):** The inmate's ID card issued by the facility is usually the standard acceptable identification. Scrutinize it carefully and record all the details (ID type, issuing agency, ID number) in your notary journal. If the facility does not issue IDs, confirm what alternative identification methods are permitted by your state (e.g., credible witness, though this is rare and complex in a jail setting).

The Notary's Safety First: Trusting Your Gut:

- **The Challenge:** Notarizing in a jail can be an intimidating and potentially unpredictable environment. Your personal safety is your absolute number one priority.
- **Best Practices:**
  - **Prioritize Safety Above All Else:** If you feel unsafe at any point (e.g., due to an agitated inmate, a hostile environment, or a general sense of unease), politely excuse yourself and leave. Document the refusal in your notary journal and notify your commissioning authority of the situation. Never compromise your safety for a notarization fee.
  - **No Outside Items:** Strictly follow all rules regarding items you can bring into the facility (e.g., no cell phones, specific pens, no personal bags). Be prepared to leave most of your usual mobile notary supplies (except your journal and stamp) in your vehicle.
  - **Document Everything Meticulously:** Your notary journal is your shield here. Note the facility name and location in your journal, along with the inmate's ID and any other pertinent details. If you refuse, document the specific reason for refusal.

IV. Notarizing Documents in Foreign Languages

Notaries frequently encounter documents written entirely in languages they do not understand. This presents specific challenges and strict limitations that require you to be a pro at knowing and diligently adhering to your legal boundaries.

The Challenge: The Language Barrier and Your Boundaries:

- **The Challenge:** You, as the notary, cannot read the document's content. This makes it impossible for you to ascertain if it contains blank spaces, appears fraudulent, or if the notarial certificate wording is compliant with your state's laws. Your notary commission **does not** grant you the authority to interpret or translate legal documents. Overstepping this boundary is a direct violation of UPL (Unauthorized Practice of Law).
- **Best Practices:**
    - **Notarize the Signature, Not the Content:** This is your unwavering mantra! Your seal and signature attest *only* to the identity of the signer and the performance of the notarial act (e.g., that they acknowledged their signature), **not** to the content, truthfulness, legality, or effectiveness of the foreign language document. Make this distinction crystal clear to the signer.
    - **Signer Must Understand:** The signer **must** understand the document they are signing. You should confirm this with the signer. If the signer explicitly states they do not understand the document, you **must** refuse.
    - **No Notary Translation or Interpretation:** Never attempt to translate or interpret the document for the signer, even if you have some proficiency in the language. This is UPL. Your role is ministerial, not advisory.
    - **Translator's Affidavit (if applicable):** If a translation is needed, you can notarize a separate

affidavit from a **qualified, impartial translator** who swears or affirms to the accuracy of their translation. In this scenario, you are notarizing the *translator's signature on the affidavit*, not the translation itself or the original foreign document. The translator must be present and identified.
  - **Journal Entry:** Clearly note in your journal that the document was in a foreign language (e.g., "Power of Attorney, Spanish language"). This provides a clear record of the document's nature.

Foreign Documents and Apostilles (Revisiting Chapter 3 of *Notary Niche Navigator*):

- **The Challenge:** A foreign document, even if notarized in the U.S., may need an Apostille or Authentication to be legally recognized in another country. Your signature and seal are only one part of that multi-step process.
- **Best Practices:**
  - **Know Your Role:** Remember your role is to perform the initial notarization accurately. Your signature and seal are what the Secretary of State (or other designated authority) will then authenticate. You are not responsible for the entire Apostille process unless you are offering it as a separate facilitation service (as discussed in *Notary Niche Navigator*).
  - **Consult:** If you have questions about the Apostille process, the specific requirements for foreign documents, or whether a document is eligible for an Apostille, consult your state's Notary Handbook or the resources we've discussed in our books. You can also refer the client to an Apostille service provider or the relevant embassy/consulate.

V. The Notary's Guiding Principle: Protecting Autonomy and "When in Doubt, Don't"

In all complex legal scenarios, especially those involving disabilities, high-risk environments, or foreign languages, the notary's guiding principle must be to **protect the signer's autonomy and dignity** above all else. This means your unwavering vigilance ensures that the notarization reflects the true, unhindered will of the signer. And if you're ever in doubt, the best advice I can give you, a mantra I live by, is simple, powerful, and absolutely non-negotiable: **"When in doubt, don't."** This phrase is your ultimate protection.

The Consequences of Overstepping: A Reminder of the Stakes: Ignoring your guiding principle or compromising your duties in these complex scenarios can lead to severe repercussions, as we've explored throughout the "Notary Knowledge" series, particularly in *Notary Law & Liability* and *Notary Fraud Shield.*

- **UPL (Unauthorized Practice of Law):** Providing advice or performing acts outside your commission can lead to civil lawsuits, criminal charges, and commission revocation.
- **Invalid Notarization:** Rendering the document void, causing significant legal problems and delays for clients.
- **Liability:** Facing substantial civil lawsuits for damages, criminal charges (e.g., for official misconduct or aiding fraud), and administrative penalties (fines, suspension, revocation of commission).
- **Harm to Public:** Directly enabling fraud or the exploitation of vulnerable individuals, a betrayal of your public trust.
- **Reputational Damage:** Irreparably damaging your professional standing and business.

The Power of Referral: Guiding Clients to the Right Help: When you encounter a scenario that is beyond your scope or comfort level, the most professional and ethical practice is to refer the client to the appropriate professional. This doesn't mean you're losing business; it means you're building trust and demonstrating your expertise in knowing your boundaries.

- **Refer to an Attorney:** When a scenario is beyond your scope (e.g., requires legal advice, document drafting, or questions about legal capacity), refer the client to a licensed attorney for proper legal counsel.
- **Refer to an Issuing Agency:** For certified copies of vital records (birth, death, marriage certificates), always refer the client to the official government agency that issued the document.
- **Refer to Another Notary:** If you have a conflict of interest, or if you are not commissioned for a specific act (e.g., RON, or a specialized niche you don't offer), refer them to another impartial, qualified notary who can assist. This builds goodwill within the notary community.
- **Refer to a Qualified Translator:** For foreign language documents where a certified translation is required, refer the client to a professional, impartial translator.

Conclusion

Navigating complex legal scenarios is an honor and a privilege. It's a true test of your compassion, patience, and unwavering adherence to professional standards. By understanding how to accommodate signers with special needs, and by steadfastly refusing to compromise on your assessment of awareness and willingness, you fulfill your vital role as an indispensable guardian of trust. Your commitment to protecting the autonomy and dignity of every individual, regardless of their circumstances, is a testament to your professional integrity and a cornerstone of your service. So go forth, my fellow notary, with a compassionate heart and a meticulous mind, and continue to make a profound difference in the lives of those you serve. The future of notarization is filled with incredible opportunities to serve in ways we've never imagined, and I can't wait to see what you do!

Chapter 6: The Notary as a Leader: Vision, Ethics, and The Next Generation

Okay, my amazing fellow notary and future leader! It's me, Derrick Spruill, and I am absolutely thrilled to bring you to this penultimate chapter of **"The Future Notary: Mastering RON, eNotary, and Complex Scenarios."** We've navigated the thrilling digital frontiers of RON and eNotary, embracing technology with open arms. We've grounded ourselves in the profound human dignity of serving those with disabilities and confidently tackled the challenges of high-risk environments. Now, it's time to take a step back and look at the bigger picture, to understand that our role extends far beyond a single notarization. We are more than just professionals who authenticate documents; we are a vital pillar of our communities, entrusted with a sacred public trust, and poised to lead. This chapter is about embracing your inherent role as a **leader**—one who actively shapes the future of the notary profession through your personal vision, your unwavering ethical conduct, and your profound commitment to mentoring and inspiring the next generation. Get ready to build a legacy that truly shines!

I. Introduction: The Legacy You Build

My journey with Mobile Notary by Derrick Spruill, operating out of Herndon, Virginia, has been one of continuous evolution. It began with a simple desire to serve, then grew into a thriving business, and has since expanded into a profound passion for empowering and educating other notaries through the "Notary Knowledge by Derrick Spruill" podcast and this entire comprehensive book series. This evolution taught me that every notarization you perform, every act of diligence, and every moment you choose to uphold integrity is not just a job—it's an integral part of the lasting legacy you build. It's about making a positive difference that extends far beyond a single transaction or a single client interaction. It's about contributing to something larger than yourself, something that endures.

My Journey from Notary to Educator: I've learned that the true essence of expertise is not just having knowledge, but generously sharing it with others. The "why" behind my podcast and my books is simple and heartfelt: I deeply believe that a vibrant community of highly skilled, ethical, and knowledgeable notaries is our best collective defense against fraud and our greatest asset in faithfully serving the public. My personal mantra, "Right Now, I'm Right Where I'm Supposed to Be," applies not only to my individual appointments but also to this inspiring mission of mentorship and education. I'm here to inspire you to recognize and embrace your potential as a leader in your own right, right in your own community. It's a joyful calling to uplift, guide, and illuminate the path for others, helping them avoid the pitfalls I encountered and achieve their own notary dreams. There's immense satisfaction in seeing another notary thrive because of knowledge you shared.

How Your Individual Practice Impacts the Profession's Future: Each notarization you perform is not a solitary act; it is a public act, a direct interaction with the legal and commercial fabric of our society. When you perform it with impeccable professionalism, unwavering diligence, and absolute integrity, you powerfully reinforce the public's trust in our entire profession. This builds a collective reputation that benefits every notary. Conversely, when an error occurs, or worse, when there's an instance of misconduct (as we explored in *Notary Law & Liability* and *Notary Fraud Shield*), it unfortunately chips away at that precious trust, impacting all notaries. Your individual practice is a direct reflection of our collective profession, and your unwavering commitment to excellence is precisely what will ultimately secure our place as indispensable public servants in the future. You are a living testament to the profession's value, and your actions, big or small, contribute to its overall standing.

II. The Notary as a Professional and Entrepreneur

Your notary commission is not merely a credential; it is the robust foundation of a professional enterprise, a business you build with your own hands and heart. Embracing both the professional duties (your public officer role) and the entrepreneurial spirit (your business owner role) of your position is key to building a practice that is not only compliant and ethical but also resilient, innovative, and profoundly successful. It's about finding that sweet spot where public service meets profitable business.

Cultivating Your Professional Reputation: Your reputation is, without a doubt, your most valuable asset. It's what clients read about in your glowing Google reviews (as I've been blessed to receive for Mobile Notary by Derrick Spruill) and what discerning referral sources eagerly share with their networks. A stellar reputation is meticulously built on a foundation of unwavering consistency: punctuality, meticulous preparedness, impeccable professionalism in every interaction, and a seamless, positive client experience. It's about showing up, being ready, and delivering excellence every single time. Your reputation is your personal brand, and it is a powerful, organic force for attracting high-value business and fostering enduring trust. It's the silent salesperson working for you 24/7.

A Notary's Strategic Vision: Every great leader has a clear, inspiring vision. What is yours for your notary practice? Is it to be the undisputed go-to Loan Signing Agent in your county, known for flawless closings and exceptional document handling? The expert in Apostille services for your state's international community, connecting local documents to global opportunities with ease? Or the compassionate notary who specializes in serving vulnerable clients in hospitals and care facilities, bringing dignity and peace of mind when it's needed most? By developing a clear strategic vision for your practice, you can precisely focus your training, your marketing efforts, and your business development strategies to achieve true niche dominance (a topic we explored in *Notary Niche Navigator*). Your vision guides your growth, giving purpose and direction to every decision.

Embracing Technology as a Tool for Service and Growth: Technology, as we've seen throughout *The Notary Future*, is not a looming threat; it's a magnificent tool for enhanced service and accelerated growth. By mastering cutting-edge innovations like Remote Online Notarization (RON) and the efficiencies of Electronic Notarization (eNotary), you not only expand your reach exponentially (serving clients across states or even globally!) but also powerfully demonstrate that you are a modern, forward-thinking professional who is ready to meet and exceed the demands of the digital age. Your ability to seamlessly integrate new technology into your practice positions you as an innovative leader, appealing to a broader, more diverse, and often more lucrative clientele who value speed, security, and convenience. It's about leveraging the best tools to deliver the best service.

III. The Notary as an Ethical Compass

You are a public officer, entrusted with a sacred duty, and your personal ethics directly and profoundly impact your public role. A notary who consistently acts as an ethical compass for their community is a leader in the truest and most impactful sense of the word. Your integrity is the light that guides your path and inspires others.

Living Your Values: Integrity Above All: Your unwavering commitment to integrity is paramount. In my life, and in every facet of my business, this is profoundly guided by my love for my Lord and Savior Jesus Christ. I deeply believe that true service, authentic professionalism, and lasting impact flow directly from a heart dedicated to higher principles. This belief is reflected in my unwavering commitment to impartiality, absolute honesty, meticulous diligence, and the courage to do what is right, always, even when it's difficult. As a notary, your integrity is not just a principle; it is your ultimate currency, your unshakeable foundation. It is what allows you to stand firm in the face of pressure and confidently refuse an improper notarization (as we discussed in *Notary Fraud Shield*), knowing you are upholding a higher standard and protecting the innocent.

Mentoring New Notaries: Sharing Knowledge and Best Practices: The future, the very longevity and strength of our noble profession, depends entirely on the next generation of notaries. A true leader doesn't hoard knowledge; they generously share it, offering support and guidance. Consider actively connecting with aspiring notaries in your community, sharing your experiences, offering practical tips, and enthusiastically guiding them toward the right resources (like this very book series!). By doing so, you elevate not just yourself, but the entire profession, fostering a vibrant culture of excellence, mutual support, and shared wisdom. It's a joyful way to pay it forward and ensure our profession continues to thrive.

Promoting a Culture of Compliance: Your unwavering dedication to meticulously following the law is a powerful act of leadership. By consistently adhering to state regulations, strictly avoiding the Unauthorized Practice of Law (UPL), and acting as an impeccable example of operational excellence, you actively promote and strengthen a culture of compliance that reinforces our collective public trust. You are a sentinel of legal boundaries, a guardian of the rules, and that is a leadership role of immense importance. Your consistent example inspires others to follow suit, creating a ripple effect of responsible and ethical practice throughout the notary community.

IV. The World of Little Notary Derrick: Inspiring the Next Generation

This vital mission of mentorship and education extends beautifully beyond just adult notaries. It's also about joyfully inspiring the next generation, instilling core values from a young age, and showing them the positive impact of public service. That's the heartwarming vision behind "Little Notary Derrick Children's Books" and "Learning with Derrick Activity Books."

The Vision Behind the Children's Books: My "Little Notary Derrick Children's Books" series is playfully aimed at helping kids with reading, alphabet, math, and solving puzzles. But the real, deeper purpose is to gently introduce the core values of integrity, trust, honesty, and public service at an early, formative age. I want to make the role of the notary relatable, understandable, and inspiring for children, fostering an intrinsic understanding of these timeless principles that are crucial not just for any future profession, but for life itself. It's about planting seeds of good character, showing them that even seemingly small acts of diligence and honesty contribute to a greater good. Imagine a child learning about the importance of a "true copy" or "honest signature" from Little Notary Derrick!

How Fostering Integrity Early Strengthens the Future: By making the notary profession accessible, fun, and meaningful for children, we are actively laying the groundwork for a future generation that intuitively understands and values the importance of integrity, honesty, and civic duty. It's a joyful and proactive way to build a lasting legacy that extends far beyond our own notary practice, shaping a more trustworthy and responsible society for tomorrow. It's a beautiful investment in the future, ensuring that the principles we hold dear are passed down and cherished by those who will eventually lead.

V. Conclusion

The notary profession is not just about a stamp and a signature. It is about a rich, inspiring history, a present-day unwavering commitment to service, and an exciting, boundless future. It is about leadership, integrity, and the continuous, joyful pursuit of excellence. By embracing all the profound lessons in this comprehensive series—from the notary's unshakeable foundation to the impenetrable fraud shield, from the strategic business blueprint to the thrilling digital future—you are not just building a business; you are building a lasting legacy of trust and service. You are a leader, a sentinel, and a guardian of trust. The future of notarization is incredibly bright, and you are a vital, indispensable part of it. Now go forth, serve with confidence, and make your mark, knowing you are truly making a difference!

Chapter 7: The Notary Knowledge Series: A Lifelong Commitment to Excellence

Hello, my incredible fellow notary, and congratulations! It's me, Derrick Spruill, and I am absolutely overflowing with joy and pride as we reach the culmination of **"The Future Notary: Mastering RON, eNotary, and Complex Scenarios,"** and indeed, the entire **"Notary Knowledge: The Complete Guide Series."** What a magnificent, transformative journey we've shared together! From the very first page of *Notary Knowledge: Reference Guide & Notary Bible* to this final chapter, my mission has been to empower you, to inspire you, and to equip you with everything you need to build a truly exceptional, resilient, and thriving notary practice. This isn't just an ending; it's a magnificent new beginning for your professional legacy, a launchpad for your continued triumphs!

I. Introduction: Celebrating Our Journey Together – The Full Notary Knowledge Series

When I started Mobile Notary by Derrick Spruill in Herndon, Virginia, and later launched my "Notary Knowledge by Derrick Spruill" podcast, my heart's deepest desire was to share the profound lessons, the joyous discoveries, and even the challenging moments I'd learned from my own entrepreneurial journey. I wanted to help others navigate the complexities and seize the incredible opportunities in our profession. This book series, born from that heartfelt desire and fueled by the timeless values instilled by my beloved parents and the unwavering love and support of my incredible wife, is a testament to that vision. We've built this knowledge fortress brick by brick, and now, you stand ready to face any challenge and embrace every triumph.

My Personal Reflection on the Entire Series: As I look back at the scope of these eight books, I feel a tremendous sense of accomplishment, not just for having written them, but for the vibrant community of notaries I know they will serve. This series represents years of experience, countless hours of meticulous research, and a deep, abiding faith in the profound importance of our profession. It's a reflection of my personal mantra, "Right Now, I'm Right Where I'm Supposed to Be," because every word, every tip, every story, has been shared with you from a place of genuine purpose and heartfelt desire to see you succeed. I truly believe that by equipping you with this comprehensive knowledge, we are collectively elevating the entire notary profession to new heights of professionalism and public trust.

The Vision Behind Creating a Comprehensive Guide: My vision for this series was crystal clear: to create the ultimate, all-encompassing resource that leaves no notary behind. I wanted to move beyond fragmented information and provide a seamless, interconnected learning experience, a true curriculum for notary mastery. Each book was designed to build upon the last, like layers of a strong, unshakeable foundation, ensuring that by the time you reached this final volume, you possessed a complete and powerful understanding of every facet of notary work. This wasn't just about giving you answers; it was about teaching you *how to think* like an expert notary, *how to act* with operational excellence, and *how to protect* yourself and the public with unwavering integrity.

The Power of Continuous Learning: The notary profession is a living, breathing entity, constantly evolving with new technologies, changing laws, and emerging client needs. The moment we stop learning is the moment we become vulnerable, stagnant, and risk falling behind. This series is a powerful starting point, a magnificent launchpad, but it's also a testament to the power of continuous learning. My unwavering commitment to staying updated, through my podcast and website, is a direct result of this belief. I want to inspire you to embrace lifelong learning as your greatest competitive advantage, your most profound professional joy, and the secret to a resilient, future-proofed career. It's an adventure that never truly ends!

II. The Pillars of Your Notary Knowledge: A Series Recap

Let's take a moment, a joyful pause, to reflect on the incredible tapestry of knowledge we've meticulously woven throughout this entire series. Each book, each chapter, each lesson, has contributed an indispensable thread to building your complete notary toolkit, preparing you not just for the present, but for a future of unparalleled service, unwavering confidence, and resounding success.

The Unshakeable Foundation (*The Notary Public Foundation: Your Essential Guide to Core Duties, Ethics, and Commissioning*): Our grand journey began with *The Notary Public Foundation.* Here, we didn't just scratch the surface; we laid the bedrock, understanding the rich historical roots of our noble profession, tracing its lineage from ancient scribes to modern-day guardians of trust. We meticulously defined the core notarial acts, embracing the absolute necessity of impartiality and unwavering ethics, and meticulously navigating the state-specific commissioning process. You learned that your commission is more than a license; it's a profound public trust, a sacred oath, and the unshakeable starting point for everything you do. This book gave you the unshakeable confidence to step boldly into your vital role, understanding the very essence of what it means to be a Notary Public. It's where your journey truly began, grounded in timeless principles.

Precision in Practice (*Notary Operational Excellence: Mastering Certificates, Journals, Ink, and Copy Certification*): Next, we honed your skills to a razor-sharp edge with *Notary Operational Excellence*. This is where precision truly became your superpower! We dove deep into flawlessly completing notarial certificates, understanding every blank and every required phrase. We mastered maintaining your notary journal as your primary defense, recognizing its power as an irrefutable audit trail against any challenge. We explored the subtle yet critical importance of ink color, ensuring your marks are permanent and tamper-evident. And we navigated the nuanced world of copy certification, understanding its limitations and best practices. You learned that true excellence is found in the meticulous execution of every single detail, safeguarding both your commission and the integrity of every document you touch. This book transformed your good intentions into flawless, repeatable execution.

Your Fortress Against Fraud (*Notary Fraud Shield: Real-World Tactics, Red Flags, and Refusal Strategies*): Then came the crucial defense, a vital armor for any modern notary: *Notary Fraud Shield*. This book didn't just inform; it powerfully armed you against the cunning, ever-evolving tactics of fraudsters. We meticulously unmasked identity deception, learned to spot subtle signs of document manipulation, recognized insidious psychological ploys, and, most importantly, embraced the unwavering power of refusal as your ultimate, non-negotiable defense. You are now equipped to be a formidable guardian of trust, a vigilant sentinel protecting the public and yourself from exploitation and deception. This book gave you the courage to say "no" when it matters most, turning you into a proactive force for good.

The Blueprint for Your Business Empire (*The Mobile Notary Blueprint: Launching and Managing Your On-Demand Business*): With your core skills and fraud shield firmly in place, we enthusiastically shifted to entrepreneurship with *The Mobile Notary Blueprint*. This was your exhilarating guide to transforming your commission into a thriving, flexible, and profitable enterprise! We covered establishing your robust legal and financial foundations, meticulously equipping your mobile office for on-the-go excellence, strategically pricing your services for optimal profit, mastering efficient scheduling and seamless logistics, and delivering an exceptional client experience that keeps them coming back. You now have the comprehensive roadmap to build a resilient and profitable business that truly serves your community. This book turned your notary commission into a powerful engine for success, showing you how to be both a public servant and a savvy entrepreneur.

Navigating Specialized Opportunities (*Notary Niche Navigator: Your Guide to Loan Signings, Apostilles, I-9s, and More*): Our adventure continued into the exciting world of specialization with *Notary Niche Navigator*. This book showed you how to unlock significantly higher income and become an indispensable expert by mastering lucrative niches like complex loan signings, intricate Apostille services for international documents, and crucial I-9 verifications. You learned to confidently serve critical legal and estate needs, and to strategically expand your portfolio with a myriad of everyday and complementary services, truly building your specialized niche empire. This is where your expertise truly shines, allowing you to find your unique place in the market and command premium fees for your specialized value.

Mastering Legal Boundaries (*Notary Law & Liability: Understanding State Regulations, Insurance, and Avoiding UPL*): Just before this book, we solidified your legal understanding with *Notary Law & Liability*. This essential guide clarified the complex legal framework governing your duties, explored the various forms of civil, criminal, and administrative liability, and demystified the crucial role of notary bonds and indispensable E&O insurance. You learned to confidently operate within your legal scope, making every boundary an unshakeable fortress of protection for your commission and your personal assets. This book gave you the peace of mind that comes with knowing the rules, and the confidence to navigate them without fear.

Embracing Tomorrow's Notary (*The Future Notary: Mastering RON, eNotary, and Complex Scenarios*): And now, with this very book, *The Notary Future*, we've peered into the exciting horizon! We've enthusiastically embraced the digital age, mastering the revolutionary capabilities of Remote Online Notarization (RON) and the efficiency of Electronic Notarization (eNotary). We've learned to navigate sensitive situations with dignity and compassion, serving those with disabilities and in high-risk environments like hospitals and jails. You are now prepared not just for the present, but for the thrilling, ever-evolving future of notarization, ready to lead the charge! This book has made you a notary ready for tomorrow, equipped with cutting-edge skills and a forward-thinking mindset.

Your Ultimate Reference (*Notary Knowledge: Reference Guide & Notary Bible*): And let's not forget the anchor of it all, the comprehensive volume that ties every thread together: *Notary Knowledge: Reference Guide & Notary Bible*. This is your ultimate desk reference, your go-to source for the overarching principles, state-specific laws, and detailed guidance that underpins every single book in this series. Keep it close, consult it often, and let it be the constant companion on your journey to notary excellence. It's the master key to your entire knowledge fortress!

III. Key Takeaways for Your Lifelong Journey

As you step forward, armed with the profound wisdom and practical strategies of the entire "Notary Knowledge: The Complete Guide Series," remember these fundamental takeaways. These are the guiding stars for your lifelong journey as an exceptional, resilient, and impactful Notary Public:

Your State Law is Your North Star: Always, always, always consult your state's official notary handbook and statutes. This is your ultimate authority, your non-negotiable guide. Laws are dynamic and constantly changing, so subscribe to updates, engage in continuous learning, and verify information regularly. It's your personal legal compass, always pointing you in the right direction, ensuring every act is compliant, legally sound, and true. This diligent adherence protects both you and the public.

Integrity is Your Ultimate Currency: Your reputation for unwavering honesty, absolute impartiality, and impeccable ethical conduct is, without a doubt, your most valuable asset. It builds profound trust with clients, attracts lucrative business, and provides an unshakeable foundation for your commission. Never, under any circumstances, compromise your integrity, even when faced with pressure, emotional appeals, or the temptation of perceived gain. It's the bedrock of your professional soul, a reflection of your character, and the essence of your public trust.

Vigilance is Your Superpower: Cultivate a keen, observant eye. Develop your ability to spot red flags—whether it's subtle identity deception, clever document manipulation, or insidious psychological ploys. Your unwavering vigilance is your most powerful tool against fraud, protecting not just your business from devastating lawsuits, but also the vulnerable public from exploitation. Be the human firewall, the sentinel who sees beyond the surface.

Service is Your Calling: Never forget the profound human element in every notarization. You are serving people, often during significant, sometimes stressful or emotional, life events. Approach each client with genuine empathy, unwavering professionalism, and a heartfelt desire to assist. Your service makes a profound difference in their lives, providing peace of mind and legal certainty, and that fulfillment is a priceless reward that enriches your own life.

Learning Never Stops: The notary profession is a vibrant, dynamic, and ever-evolving landscape. Embrace continuous learning not as a chore, but as a joyful pursuit and an exciting adventure. Stay updated on new laws, groundbreaking technologies (like RON and eNotary), emerging fraud tactics, and evolving best practices. Your commitment to ongoing education ensures you remain competent, confident, relevant, and authoritative in an ever-changing professional world. It's the secret to staying ahead of the curve.

Your Network is Your Strength: Cultivate strong, reciprocal relationships with fellow notaries, legal professionals (attorneys, paralegals), real estate agents, title company professionals, and other referral sources. Your network provides invaluable support, mentorship, a platform for sharing experiences, and a consistent source of high-quality business opportunities. We are stronger, wiser, and more resilient when we support each other.

IV. Essential Next Steps & Follow-Up Information

This series is a magnificent launchpad, not a finish line! Here's how you can continue to build on this incredible foundation and propel your notary career to new heights:

Stay Connected with Derrick Spruill:

- **Podcast:** Keep listening to the **"Notary Knowledge by Derrick Spruill" podcast** for ongoing insights, engaging interviews with industry leaders, practical tips, and timely updates on the notary world. I'm always sharing new lessons and stories there!
- **Website:** Visit `MobileNotarybyDerrickSpruill.com` regularly for updated resources, insightful blog posts, and information on my services and upcoming events.
- **Social Media:** Connect with me on LinkedIn, Facebook, and X (Twitter) for daily tips, breaking industry news, and opportunities for community engagement. I love interacting with fellow notaries!

Join Professional Associations:

- **National Notary Association (NNA):** If you haven't already, become a member of the NNA. Their resources, legal hotlines, comprehensive continuing education programs, and advocacy efforts are invaluable.

- **State Notary Associations:** Seek out and join your state's specific notary association. They provide localized support, critical updates relevant to your jurisdiction, and networking opportunities with notaries in your area.

Seek Specialized Training:

- **Loan Signing Agent (LSA):** If you're ready to dive into the lucrative world of real estate closings, pursue LSA certification from a reputable provider.
- **Remote Online Notarization (RON):** If your state permits, get commissioned and trained on an approved RON platform to expand your digital services.
- **Other Niches:** Explore training for Apostille services, fingerprinting, or other specialized areas that align with your business vision.

Keep Your Reference Guide Handy:

- Always keep your **"Notary Knowledge: Reference Guide & Notary Bible"** close by. It's designed to be your ultimate, quick-reference companion for all overarching notary principles and state-specific laws.

Embrace the Little Notary Derrick Vision:

- Consider exploring the "Little Notary Derrick Children's Books" and "Learning with Derrick Activity Books." It's a joyful way to reinforce core values of integrity and service, not just for children, but as a reminder for all of us about the simple, profound truths of our profession.

V. A Final, Heartfelt Message of Empowerment

My fellow notary, you have embarked on an extraordinary, impactful path. Your unwavering commitment to public service, your dedication to continuous learning, and your profound passion for upholding integrity are truly inspiring. I want you to feel the immense pride and profound satisfaction that comes with being a Notary Public. You are an indispensable part of our legal and commercial fabric. You are a guardian of trust, a formidable fraud shield, a savvy entrepreneur, and a beacon of professionalism in your community.

Remember my personal mantra: **"Right Now, I'm Right Where I'm Supposed to Be."** Embrace that powerful feeling in your own notary journey. Let it fuel your passion, guide your decisions, and illuminate your path. Every challenge is an exhilarating opportunity to learn and grow, every client is a cherished opportunity to serve with excellence, and every notarization is a profound opportunity to make a positive, lasting impact on someone's life.

Go forth with boundless confidence, with a joyful and open heart, and with the full knowledge that you are equipped for unparalleled excellence. The future of notarization is incredibly bright, filled with magnificent possibilities, and I can't wait to see the amazing things you will accomplish!

Thank you for allowing me to be your guide through this extraordinary series. It has been an honor and a privilege, and I look forward to witnessing your continued success.

Bonus Chapter: Your Digital Compass: Finding RON & eNotary Laws and Providers by State

Hello, my incredible fellow notary and digital pioneer! It's me, Derrick Spruill, and I'm absolutely thrilled to bring you this special bonus chapter for **"The Future Notary : Mastering RON, eNotary, and Complex Scenarios."** Throughout this book, we've explored the exhilarating landscape of Remote Online Notarization (RON) and

Electronic Notarization (eNotary), and I know your mind is buzzing with the possibilities! You're ready to dive in, to expand your reach, and to serve clients in ways you never imagined.

My journey with Mobile Notary by Derrick Spruill, operating out of Herndon, Virginia, and my constant research for the "Notary Knowledge by Derrick Spruill" podcast, means I spend a fair amount of time on these state websites. I've learned a few tricks, and my goal in this bonus chapter is to empower you to confidently find the exact RON and eNotary laws, requirements, and, most importantly, the **state-approved technology providers** for your specific jurisdiction. Think of this chapter as your personal digital compass, always pointing you to the most current and accurate information!

I. The Power of Proactive Research: Why Knowing Where to Look Matters

The digital notarization landscape is a vibrant, ever-evolving ecosystem. New laws are passed, regulations are updated, and technology providers gain (or lose) state approval. Your commitment to continuous learning means you need to know *how* to access these primary sources directly. This isn't just about compliance; it's about giving you the tools to be proactive, informed, and truly excel in this exciting new frontier. It's about empowering you to be a master of your own digital destiny!

Your State's Commissioning Authority: Your Digital Beacon: The first and most crucial piece of information you need is your state's **commissioning authority**. In almost all U.S. states, this is the **Secretary of State's office** or an equivalent department (like the Lieutenant Governor's Office or Department of Licensing). Their website is your primary destination for all notary-related information, including specific guidance on RON and eNotary. This is your official, trusted source – always start here!

Key Terms to Search For on State Websites: Once you're on the correct state government website, use their internal search function with these keywords. You're looking for their "RON Notary

Handbook," "eNotary Registration," or a list of "Approved RON Providers."

- "Remote Online Notarization (RON)"
- "Electronic Notarization (eNotary)"
- "Online Notary"
- "Digital Notary"
- "Approved RON Providers" or "Approved eNotary Vendors"
- "Notary Handbook" (and then look for sections on electronic/online notarization)

Always look for the most current version of the handbook or statutes, often indicated by a "last updated" date or a specific edition year. This ensures you're working with the latest rules!

II. State-by-State Guide: Finding RON & eNotary Laws and Approved Providers Online (50 States + DC)

Here's your detailed, state-by-state guide on how to typically locate the official RON and eNotary laws and resources for each state. Remember, website interfaces can change, but the core department responsible for notary services usually remains the same. My goal is to give you a clear starting point for your own proactive research, empowering you to find the most up-to-date information directly from the source!

Disclaimer: The landscape of RON and eNotary is dynamic. State laws, regulations, and lists of approved technology providers are subject to frequent change. The information below provides the **official state website** as your primary resource. **It is absolutely essential and non-negotiable for all prospective RON or eNotary Publics to verify the most current and precise requirements and the definitive list of approved technology providers directly with their respective state's commissioning authority's website before initiating any commissioning process or performing any digital notarization.** Relying on outdated information can lead to non-compliance, invalid notarizations, and severe penalties.

Alabama

- **Commissioning Authority:** Alabama Secretary of State
- **Website:** `https://www.sos.alabama.gov/`
- **How to Find:** Navigate to "Government Records" or "Business Services," then look for "Notary Public" or directly search for "Remote Online Notarization."
- **Providers:** The AL SOS website will list approved RON technology providers.

Alaska

- **Commissioning Authority:** Alaska Lieutenant Governor's Office
- **Website:** `https://ltgov.alaska.gov/`
- **How to Find:** Look for "Notary Public" or "Elections & Notaries," then find information on "Online Notary."
- **Providers:** The AK Lt. Gov. website will list approved RON technology providers.

Arizona

- **Commissioning Authority:** Arizona Secretary of State
- **Website:** `https://azsos.gov/`
- **How to Find:** Search for "Notary Public" or look under "Services," then find "Online Notary."
- **Providers:** The AZ SOS website will list approved RON technology providers.

Arkansas

- **Commissioning Authority:** Arkansas Secretary of State
- **Website:** `https://www.sos.arkansas.gov/`
- **How to Find:** Look for "Notary Public & Apostilles" or directly search for "Remote Online Notarization."
- **Providers:** The AR SOS website will list approved RON technology providers.

California

- **Commissioning Authority:** California Secretary of State
- **Website:** `https://www.sos.ca.gov/`
- **How to Find:** Navigate to "Notary Public" under "Business Programs" or "Divisions."
- **Status: RON is NOT currently permitted in California.** While temporary measures existed during the pandemic, permanent RON legislation has not yet been enacted. Keep an eye on this page for future updates!
- **Providers:** N/A.

Colorado

- **Commissioning Authority:** Colorado Secretary of State
- **Website:** `https://www.sos.state.co.us/`
- **How to Find:** Look for "Notaries Public" under "Business & Licensing," then find "Online Notary."
- **Providers:** The CO SOS website will list approved RON technology providers.

Connecticut

- **Commissioning Authority:** Connecticut Secretary of State
- **Website:** `https://portal.ct.gov/sots`
- **How to Find:** Look for "Notary Public" under "Business Services" or "Commissions," then find "Online Notary."
- **Providers:** The CT SOS website will list approved RON technology providers.

Delaware

- **Commissioning Authority:** Delaware Secretary of State
- **Website:** `https://corp.delaware.gov/`
- **How to Find:** Search for "Notary Public" or look under "Services," then find "Online Notary."
- **Providers:** The DE SOS website will list approved RON technology providers.

District of Columbia

- **Commissioning Authority:** DC Mayor's Office (Office of Notary Commissions and Authentications)
- **Website:** `https://os.dc.gov/page/notary-commissions-and-authentications`
- **How to Find:** Look for "Online Notary" or "Remote Notarization."
- **Providers:** The DC OS website will list approved RON technology providers.

Florida

- **Commissioning Authority:** Florida Department of State
- **Website:** `https://dos.myflorida.com/`
- **How to Find:** Look for "Notaries Public" under "Divisions" or "Business Services," then find "Online Notary Public." Florida was a pioneer in RON, so their resources are extensive!
- **Providers:** The FL DOS website will list approved RON technology providers.

Georgia

- **Commissioning Authority:** Georgia Superior Court Clerks' Cooperative Authority (GSCCCA)
- **Website:** `https://www.gsccca.org/`
- **How to Find:** Look for "Notary Public" and then "Electronic Notarization" or "Remote Online Notarization."
- **Providers:** The GSCCCA website will list approved RON technology providers.

Hawaii

- **Commissioning Authority:** Hawaii Attorney General's Office
- **Website:** `https://ag.hawaii.gov/`
- **How to Find:** Search for "Notary Public" and then "Electronic Notarization" or "Remote Online Notarization."
- **Providers:** The HI AG website will list approved RON technology providers.

Idaho

- **Commissioning Authority:** Idaho Secretary of State
- **Website:** `https://sos.idaho.gov/`
- **How to Find:** Look for "Notaries" under "Business & Corporations," then find "Remote Online Notarization."
- **Providers:** The ID SOS website will list approved RON technology providers.

Illinois

- **Commissioning Authority:** Illinois Secretary of State
- **Website:** `https://www.cyberdriveillinois.com/`
- **How to Find:** Look for "Notary Public" under "Departments," then find "Electronic Notary" or "Remote Notarization."
- **Providers:** The IL SOS website will list approved RON technology providers.

Indiana

- **Commissioning Authority:** Indiana Secretary of State
- **Website:** `https://www.in.gov/sos/`
- **How to Find:** Search for "Notary Public" or look under "Business Services," then find "Remote Notary."
- **Providers:** The IN SOS website will list approved RON technology providers.

Iowa

- **Commissioning Authority:** Iowa Secretary of State
- **Website:** `https://sos.iowa.gov/`
- **How to Find:** Look for "Notary Public" under "Business Services," then find "Online Notary."
- **Providers:** The IA SOS website will list approved RON technology providers.

Kansas

- **Commissioning Authority:** Kansas Secretary of State
- **Website:** `https://www.sos.ks.gov/`
- **How to Find:** Look for "Notary Public" under "Business Services," then find "Remote Online Notarization."
- **Providers:** The KS SOS website will list approved RON technology providers.

Kentucky

- **Commissioning Authority:** Kentucky Secretary of State
- **Website:** `https://www.sos.ky.gov/`
- **How to Find:** Look for "Notary Public" under "Business," then find "Online Notary."
- **Providers:** The KY SOS website will list approved RON technology providers.

Louisiana

- **Commissioning Authority:** Louisiana Secretary of State
- **Website:** `https://www.sos.la.gov/`
- **How to Find:** Look for "Notary & Commissions" or "Commercial Division," then find "Remote Online Notarization."
- **Providers:** The LA SOS website will list approved RON technology providers.

Maine

- **Commissioning Authority:** Maine Secretary of State
- **Website:** `https://www.maine.gov/sos/`
- **How to Find:** Look for "Notary Public" under "Bureau of Corporations, Elections & Commissions," then find "Electronic Notarization" or "Remote Online Notarization."
- **Providers:** The ME SOS website will list approved RON technology providers.

Maryland

- **Commissioning Authority:** Maryland Secretary of State
- **Website:** `https://sos.state.md.us/`
- **How to Find:** Look for "Notary Public" under "Services," then find "Remote Notarization."
- **Providers:** The MD SOS website will list approved RON technology providers.

Massachusetts

- **Commissioning Authority:** Massachusetts Secretary of the Commonwealth
- **Website:** `https://www.sec.state.ma.us/`
- **How to Find:** Look for "Notary Public" under "Commissions," then find "Remote Online Notarization."
- **Providers:** The MA SOC website will list approved RON technology providers.

Michigan

- **Commissioning Authority:** Michigan Secretary of State
- **Website:** `https://www.michigan.gov/sos`
- **How to Find:** Search for "Notary Public" or look under "Business Services," then find "Remote Notarization."
- **Providers:** The MI SOS website will list approved RON technology providers.

Minnesota

- **Commissioning Authority:** Minnesota Secretary of State
- **Website:** `https://www.sos.state.mn.us/`
- **How to Find:** Look for "Notary & Apostille" under "Business & Filings," then find "Online Notary."
- **Providers:** The MN SOS website will list approved RON technology providers.

Mississippi

- **Commissioning Authority:** Mississippi Secretary of State
- **Website:** `https://www.sos.ms.gov/`
- **How to Find:** Look for "Notary Public" under "Business Services," then find "Remote Notarization."
- **Providers:** The MS SOS website will list approved RON technology providers.

Missouri

- **Commissioning Authority:** Missouri Secretary of State
- **Website:** `https://www.sos.mo.gov/`
- **How to Find:** Look for "Notary Public" under "Business & Commissions," then find "Remote Online Notarization."
- **Providers:** The MO SOS website will list approved RON technology providers.

Montana

- **Commissioning Authority:** Montana Secretary of State
- **Website:** `https://sos.mt.gov/`
- **How to Find:** Look for "Notary Public" under "Business Services," then find "Online Notary."
- **Providers:** The MT SOS website will list approved RON technology providers.

Nebraska

- **Commissioning Authority:** Nebraska Secretary of State
- **Website:** `https://sos.nebraska.gov/`
- **How to Find:** Look for "Notary Public" under "Business Services," then find "Online Notary."
- **Providers:** The NE SOS website will list approved RON technology providers.

Nevada

- **Commissioning Authority:** Nevada Secretary of State
- **Website:** `https://nvsos.gov/`
- **How to Find:** Look for "Notary Public" under "Business & Commercial Services," then find "Online Notary Public." Nevada was an early adopter of RON!
- **Providers:** The NV SOS website will list approved RON technology providers.

New Hampshire

- **Commissioning Authority:** New Hampshire Secretary of State
- **Website:** `https://www.sos.nh.gov/`
- **How to Find:** Look for "Notary Public" under "Commissions," then find "Remote Online Notarization."
- **Providers:** The NH SOS website will list approved RON technology providers.

New Jersey

- **Commissioning Authority:** New Jersey Division of Revenue and Enterprise Services (under State Treasurer)
- **Website:** `https://www.nj.gov/treasury/revenue/`
- **How to Find:** Search for "Notary Public" and then "Remote Online Notarization."
- **Providers:** The NJ Treasury website will list approved RON technology providers.

New Mexico

- **Commissioning Authority:** New Mexico Secretary of State
- **Website:** `https://www.sos.state.nm.us/`
- **How to Find:** Look for "Notary Public" under "Business Services," then find "Remote Online Notarization."
- **Providers:** The NM SOS website will list approved RON technology providers.

New York

- **Commissioning Authority:** New York Department of State
- **Website:** `https://dos.ny.gov/`
- **How to Find:** Look for "Notary Public" under "Licensing Services," then find "Electronic Notarization" or "Remote Online Notarization." New York's RON law became permanent relatively recently, so it's an exciting development!
- **Providers:** The NY DOS website will list approved RON technology providers.

North Carolina

- **Commissioning Authority:** North Carolina Secretary of State
- **Website:** `https://www.sosnc.gov/`
- **How to Find:** Look for "Notary Public" under "Divisions," then find "Electronic Notarization" or "Remote Online Notarization."
- **Providers:** The NC SOS website will list approved RON technology providers.

North Dakota

- **Commissioning Authority:** North Dakota Secretary of State
- **Website:** `https://www.sos.nd.gov/`
- **How to Find:** Look for "Notary Public" under "Business Services," then find "Online Notary."

- **Providers:** The ND SOS website will list approved RON technology providers.

Ohio

- **Commissioning Authority:** Ohio Secretary of State
- **Website:** `https://www.ohiosos.gov/`
- **How to Find:** Look for "Notary Public" under "Business & Filings," then find "Online Notary Public."
- **Providers:** The OH SOS website will list approved RON technology providers.

Oklahoma

- **Commissioning Authority:** Oklahoma Secretary of State
- **Website:** `https://www.sos.ok.gov/`
- **How to Find:** Look for "Notary Public" under "Business Filings," then find "Online Notary."
- **Providers:** The OK SOS website will list approved RON technology providers.

Oregon

- **Commissioning Authority:** Oregon Secretary of State
- **Website:** `https://sos.oregon.gov/`
- **How to Find:** Look for "Notary Public" under "Business & Non-Profits," then find "Online Notary."
- **Providers:** The OR SOS website will list approved RON technology providers.

Pennsylvania

- **Commissioning Authority:** Pennsylvania Department of State
- **Website:** `https://www.dos.pa.gov/`
- **How to Find:** Look for "Notaries" under "Commissions, Elections, and Legislation," then find "Remote Online Notarization."

- **Providers:** The PA DOS website will list approved RON technology providers.

Rhode Island

- **Commissioning Authority:** Rhode Island Secretary of State
- **Website:** `https://sos.ri.gov/`
- **How to Find:** Look for "Notary Public" under "Business Services," then find "Remote Online Notarization."
- **Providers:** The RI SOS website will list approved RON technology providers.

South Carolina

- **Commissioning Authority:** South Carolina Secretary of State
- **Website:** `https://sos.sc.gov/`
- **How to Find:** Look for "Notaries Public" under "Online Services," then find "Remote Online Notarization."
- **Providers:** The SC SOS website will list approved RON technology providers.

South Dakota

- **Commissioning Authority:** South Dakota Secretary of State
- **Website:** `https://sdsos.gov/`
- **How to Find:** Look for "Notary Public" under "Business Services," then find "Online Notary."
- **Providers:** The SD SOS website will list approved RON technology providers.

Tennessee

- **Commissioning Authority:** Tennessee Secretary of State
- **Website:** `https://sos.tn.gov/`
- **How to Find:** Search for "Notary Public" and then "Remote Online Notarization."

- **Providers:** The TN SOS website will list approved RON technology providers.

Texas

- **Commissioning Authority:** Texas Secretary of State
- **Website:** `https://www.sos.state.tx.us/`
- **How to Find:** Look for "Notary Public" under "Business & Commercial Services," then find "Online Notary Public." Texas was one of the very first states to enact RON, leading the way!
- **Providers:** The TX SOS website will list approved RON technology providers.

Utah

- **Commissioning Authority:** Utah Lieutenant Governor's Office
- **Website:** `https://lieutenantgovernor.utah.gov/`
- **How to Find:** Look for "Notary Public" under "Elections & Notaries," then find "Online Notary." Utah was also an early adopter, embracing the future!
- **Providers:** The UT Lt. Gov. website will list approved RON technology providers.

Vermont

- **Commissioning Authority:** Vermont Secretary of State
- **Website:** `https://sos.vermont.gov/`
- **How to Find:** Look for "Notary Public" under "Business & Corporations," then find "Remote Online Notarization."
- **Providers:** The VT SOS website will list approved RON technology providers.

Virginia

- **Commissioning Authority:** Virginia Secretary of the Commonwealth
- **Website:** `https://www.commonwealth.virginia.gov/`
- **How to Find:** Look for "Notary Public" under "Services," then find "Remote Online Notarization." Virginia was the very first state to pass RON legislation in 2011, truly pioneering the future!
- **Providers:** The VA SOC website will list approved RON technology providers.

Washington

- **Commissioning Authority:** Washington State Department of Licensing
- **Website:** `https://www.dol.wa.gov/`
- **How to Find:** Search for "Notary Public" and then "Remote Online Notarization."
- **Providers:** The WA DOL website will list approved RON technology providers.

West Virginia

- **Commissioning Authority:** West Virginia Secretary of State
- **Website:** `https://www.wvsos.gov/`
- **How to Find:** Look for "Notary Public" under "Business & Licensing," then find "Remote Online Notarization."
- **Providers:** The WV SOS website will list approved RON technology providers.

Wisconsin

- **Commissioning Authority:** Wisconsin Department of Financial Institutions
- **Website:** `https://dfi.wi.gov/`
- **How to Find:** Look for "Notary Public" and then "Remote Online Notarization."

- **Providers:** The WI DFI website will list approved RON technology providers.

Wyoming

- **Commissioning Authority:** Wyoming Secretary of State
- **Website:** `https://sos.wyo.gov/`
- **How to Find:** Look for "Notary Public" under "Business & Filings," then find "Online Notary."
- **Providers:** The WY SOS website will list approved RON technology providers.

III. Conclusion: Your Personal Legal Navigation Tool for the Digital Age

There you have it! Your very own compass for navigating the vast and varied landscape of state RON and eNotary laws and finding the approved technology providers. I hope this bonus chapter leaves you feeling incredibly empowered and inspired. Remember, my journey with Mobile Notary by Derrick Spruill and the "Notary Knowledge by Derrick Spruill" podcast is all about continuous learning and sharing knowledge.

By knowing *how* to find the most current and precise digital notary laws for any state, you equip yourself with an invaluable tool. This proactive approach ensures you always operate compliantly, protect your commission, and serve the public with the highest standards of integrity and confidence in this exciting new era. It's not just about avoiding mistakes; it's about confidently making every notarization a testament to your professionalism, whether it's in-person or online.

Go forth, my fellow notary, and navigate those state websites with a smile! Your commitment to staying informed is your ultimate superpower, and the digital future of notarization is waiting for your brilliant leadership!

Glossary of Key Terms

This glossary provides definitions for important terms used throughout **The Future Notary Mastering RON, eNotary, and Complex Scenarios**, offering a quick reference to the specialized vocabulary and critical concepts essential for understanding the legal framework, risks, and protections in your notary practice.

A

- **Acceptable Identification:** The specific forms of identification (e.g., current, government-issued photo ID) that a notary public is legally permitted to accept to confirm a signer's identity, as defined by state law.
- **Administrative Liability:** Disciplinary actions and penalties (e.g., fines, mandatory training, suspension, or revocation of commission) imposed by a state's commissioning authority on a notary for violating notary laws or rules.
- **Administrative Rules:** Detailed rules and regulations promulgated by state agencies (e.g., Secretary of State's office) to implement, clarify, and enforce the broader notary statutes.
- **Advance Healthcare Directive (AHD):** A legal document outlining an individual's future medical treatment decisions and/or appointing a healthcare agent.
- **Affidavits:** Written statements of fact voluntarily made and sworn to or affirmed under oath, often used as evidence in legal proceedings.
- **Affirmation:** A solemn, legally binding declaration, made under penalty of perjury, stating that a particular statement or document is true, serving as an alternative to an oath.
- **Agent (Power of Attorney):** The individual formally granted legal authority to act on behalf of another person (the "Principal") in a Power of Attorney (POA) document.
- **Altered Documents:** Documents that have been physically or digitally changed after their original creation, with the intent to deceive.

- **Application Process (Notary):** The step-by-step procedure for applying to become a Notary Public, including meeting eligibility, submitting forms, and fulfilling state requirements.
- **Apostille:** A standardized certificate issued by a designated authority in a Hague Convention member country, authenticating a document for international use.
- **Audit Trail:** A comprehensive, chronological, and verifiable record of events and actions related to a notarial act (e.g., journal entries, RON recordings), crucial for proving compliance and investigating fraud.
- **Authentication (International):** The multi-step process of legalizing a document for its legal recognition in a foreign country that is *not* a member of the Hague Apostille Convention.
- **Authorized Representative (for I-9):** An individual (often a notary) designated by an employer to complete Section 2 of Form I-9, verifying identity and employment authorization; a **non-notarial act**.
- **Auto Insurance (Commercial):** Insurance coverage for vehicles used primarily for business purposes, distinct from personal auto insurance, crucial for mobile notaries.

B

- **Background Check:** A comprehensive verification process undertaken by a state's commissioning authority to review an applicant's criminal history and other relevant public records, often mandatory for notary commissioning.
- **Behavioral Cues:** Non-verbal or verbal indicators from a signer that may signal deception, duress, or a lack of awareness.
- **Bond (Notary Bond):** A type of surety bond that many states legally require notaries public to obtain. Its primary purpose is to protect the *public* from financial harm caused by a notary's official misconduct, negligence, or errors. It is *not* insurance for the notary.

- **Bond Amounts:** The specific monetary value of a notary bond, which varies by state and represents the maximum payout for a public claim.
- **Borrowed/Shared Identification:** A fraudster tactic where a genuine identification document belonging to one person is used by another individual who resembles them.
- **Business Entity Type:** The legal classification of a business (e.g., Sole Proprietorship, LLC), impacting liability, taxation, and administrative burden.
- **Business Licenses:** Permits or registrations required by state or local governments to legally operate a business.

C

- **Certificates (Notarial):** The written statement formally executed by the Notary Public that attests to the specific facts of a notarial act, serving as official, legally recognized evidence of the notarization.
- **Certifying Copies:** A specialized notarial act (permitted in some states for specific documents) where a notary certifies that a photocopy or facsimile of an original document is a true and accurate reproduction of that original.
- **Civil Liability:** The notary's personal financial responsibility for monetary damages or financial losses caused to another party as a direct result of the notary's negligence, error, or misconduct while performing their official duties. Can lead to substantial lawsuits.
- **Coercion:** Unlawful pressure, threats, or intimidation used to force someone to sign a document against their free will. Notaries must diligently assess a signer's willingness to ensure they are not acting under coercion.
- **Commission (Notary):** The official authorization granted by a state government that legally empowers an individual to act as a Notary Public within that specific state's jurisdiction.
- **Commission Expiration Date:** The precise calendar date on which a notary's official commission legally ends.
- **Commissioning Authority:** The specific state government office, department, or agency that is legally responsible for

appointing, regulating, and overseeing Notaries Public within that state (e.g., Secretary of State's office).

- **Complicity in Fraud:** Being involved in a fraudulent act, even if unintentionally, by failing to uphold notarial duties (e.g., notarizing a fraudulent document due to negligence). This can lead to severe penalties for a notary, including criminal charges.
- **Compliance:** Adherence to all relevant laws, regulations, and ethical standards governing notary practice and business operations.
- **Confidentiality:** The strict ethical and legal obligation of a notary public to protect the privacy of their signers and the sensitive information contained within the documents they notarize.
- **Conflict of Interest:** A situation in which a notary public has a personal, financial, or familial interest in a document or transaction that they are asked to notarize, thereby compromising their impartiality. Notaries are ethically and legally required to refuse to act in such cases.
- **Consequences of Non-Compliance:** The negative outcomes (e.g., fines, lawsuits, commission suspension/revocation) that result from a notary's failure to adhere to laws and regulations.
- **Continuous Learning:** The ongoing commitment to staying updated on notary laws, best practices, and emerging fraud tactics, essential for maintaining competence and avoiding errors.
- **Contracts:** Legally binding agreements between two or more parties, often requiring notarization of signatures.
- **Copy Certification (Prohibitions):** State-specific rules that restrict or prohibit notaries from directly certifying copies of certain documents (e.g., vital records, publicly recordable documents).
- **Counterfeit ID:** A completely fabricated identification document that is designed to appear genuine but is fraudulent.
- **Credential Analysis (RON):** A sophisticated technological process primarily used in Remote Online Notarization (RON) for verifying a signer's identity by analyzing ID security features.

- **Credible Identifying Witness:** A method of identifying a signer when they lack acceptable photo identification. A notary-known, impartial witness who personally knows the signer attests to the signer's identity under oath.
- **Criminal Liability:** The notary's legal responsibility for violating state or federal criminal laws related to their notarial acts. This typically arises from intentional misconduct, fraudulent intent, or acts of gross negligence. Conviction can lead to fines, imprisonment, and commission revocation.
- **Cybersecurity Responsibility:** A notary's duty to protect their digital systems, electronic notary credentials, and client data from hacking, breaches, or unauthorized access, especially when performing Electronic Notarization (eNotary) or Remote Online Notarization (RON).

D

- **Deed:** A formal legal document that conveys or transfers ownership of real estate (property) from one party to another. Deeds are frequently notarized and are common targets for real estate fraud.
- **Deceptive Identification:** A broad term encompassing various tactics used by fraudsters to mislead a notary public about their true identity.
- **Defense Strategies (Notary):** Proactive measures, best practices, and systematic approaches that every notary public must implement to minimize their inherent risks, prevent errors, deter fraudulent attempts, and effectively protect themselves from potential liability and fraud.
- **Diligence:** The quality of performing duties with careful and persistent effort, a key ethical principle for notaries.
- **Diminished Capacity:** A state where a signer's mental ability or cognitive faculties are impaired to such an extent that it raises questions about their ability to fully understand a document or the notarial act.
- **Document Integrity:** The state of a document being complete, unaltered, authentic, and free from any fraudulent

changes. Proper notarization aims to preserve and attest to a document's integrity.

- **Document Manipulation:** Various tactics used by fraudsters to alter, fabricate, or otherwise compromise the authenticity or content of documents to facilitate fraud.
- **Document Substitution:** A fraudster tactic where a legitimate document is quickly and subtly swapped with a different, often fraudulent, document for the actual signature and notarization.
- **Due Care:** The legal expectation that a notary will perform their duties thoroughly, carefully, and with a comprehensive understanding of the laws.
- **Duress:** Unlawful pressure, coercion, threats, or intimidation used to force someone to sign a document against their free will. Notaries must identify signs of duress and refuse to notarize if present.

E

- **Education (Notary):** Mandatory or recommended training programs designed to familiarize prospective notaries with state laws, ethics, and procedures.
- **Electronic Journal (e-journal):** A digital record of notarial acts, maintained within a secure software platform, typically used in eNotary and RON.
- **Electronic Notarization (eNotary):** A notarial act performed on an electronic document where the notary applies an electronic signature/seal, with the signer in the *physical presence* of the notary.
- **Electronic Seal:** A digital representation of a notary's official seal, cryptographically bound to an electronic document.
- **Electronic Signature (e-signature):** A legally binding method of signing electronic documents, recognized by federal and state laws.
- **Eligibility Requirements (Notary):** The specific qualifications an individual must meet to be considered for appointment and commissioning as a Notary Public in a given state.

- **Employer Identification Number (EIN):** A unique nine-digit tax identification number assigned by the IRS to businesses.
- **Endorsement (Notary):** An official designation or approval for a notary to perform specific types of acts (e.g., RON).
- **Errors & Omissions (E&O) Insurance:** Professional liability insurance that directly protects the *notary* from financial loss resulting from claims of negligence, unintentional errors, or omissions in their notarial duties. It covers legal defense costs and judgments/settlements.
- **Ethical Considerations:** The fundamental moral principles, professional standards, and rules of conduct that guide a notary public's behavior and decision-making, emphasizing impartiality, honesty, diligence, and confidentiality.
- **Exam (Notary):** A formal test or assessment required by some states for notary applicants to assess their knowledge of notary law and procedures.
- **Exploiting Vulnerability:** A broad fraudster tactic that involves targeting individuals (e.g., the elderly, the ill) or systemic weaknesses to compromise a transaction.

F

- **Fabricated Documents:** Documents that are entirely fake or counterfeit, created from scratch by fraudsters to appear legitimate.
- **False Authority/Intimidation:** A fraudster tactic where an individual asserts a false position of power or uses aggressive language/threats to pressure a notary into bypassing proper procedures.
- **Falsifying Records:** The illegal act of intentionally altering, creating, or destroying official records, such as notary journal entries or notarial certificates, with intent to deceive. This is a criminal offense for notaries.
- **Fees (Notary):** The maximum allowable charges a notary can levy for performing notarial acts, strictly regulated by state law.

- **Filing Commission:** The process of registering a notary's commission and bond (if applicable) with a county or state office to make it active.
- **Financial Fraud:** Fraudulent schemes specifically aimed at obtaining money, assets, or financial benefits through deception, often involving fraudulent notarized documents.
- **Financial Protection:** Safeguards (e.g., E&O insurance) that shield a notary's personal and business assets from financial loss due to claims or lawsuits.
- **Forged Identification:** Identification documents that have been altered (e.g., photo substitution, data alteration) or created fraudulently to impersonate another individual.
- **Forged Signatures:** Signatures that are not genuine, created fraudulently by someone other than the rightful signer.
- **Form I-9 (Employment Eligibility Verification):** A USCIS form for employers to verify the identity and employment authorization of new hires.
- **Fraud Prevention:** The active, diligent measures employed by notaries public to deter, detect, and ultimately prevent fraudulent activities that involve documents, signatures, or identity theft.
- **Fraudster Tactics:** The various deceptive methods, manipulative techniques, and exploitative strategies used by individuals or organized criminal rings to trick notaries or bypass safeguards.
- **"Friendly Favor" Trap:** A common fraudster tactic appealing to a notary's desire to be helpful to bypass crucial rules (e.g., personal appearance).
- **Frontline Defense:** The notary's critical position as the first point of protection and interception against fraud in many legal and financial transactions.

G

- **General Liability Insurance:** Business insurance protecting against claims of bodily injury or property damage to a third party during business operations, distinct from E&O insurance.

- **Government-Issued Photo ID:** Official identification documents (e.g., driver's license, passport) issued by a government authority, required for satisfactory identification.
- **Gross Negligence:** A conscious and voluntary disregard of the need to use reasonable care, which is likely to cause foreseeable grave injury or harm to persons, property, or both. Can lead to criminal liability.
- **Guidance (Legal):** Professional counsel or interpretation of law, which notaries are prohibited from providing.

H

- **Hague Apostille Convention:** An international treaty that simplifies the authentication of public documents for their legal recognition and use in foreign countries that are also signatory members.
- **High-Value Transactions:** Transactions involving substantial monetary amounts (e.g., real estate purchases, large loans) that are particularly frequent and attractive targets for fraudsters.
- **Human Firewall:** A metaphor describing the notary's crucial role in using their human judgment, observational skills, and ethical resolve to detect and prevent fraud that technology alone might miss.

I

- **Identity Deception:** A broad term encompassing all tactics used by fraudsters to mislead a notary public about their true identity.
- **Identity Theft:** The fraudulent acquisition and unauthorized use of a person's private identifying information for financial gain, criminal activity, or other illicit purposes.
- **Identity Verification:** The notary's critical duty to confirm the signer's true identity through satisfactory evidence (e.g., valid photo ID).
- **Illegible Seal/Signature:** Notary marks (seal impression or signature) that are unclear, smudged, partial, or unreadable.

This can lead to document rejection and may indicate negligence.

- **Immigration Reform and Control Act (IRCA) of 1986:** A U.S. federal law that made it illegal for employers to knowingly hire or continue to employ unauthorized workers, mandating the use of Form I-9.
- **Impartiality:** The fundamental ethical principle and legal requirement for a notary to remain completely unbiased, neutral, and objective in every notarial act.
- **Impersonation:** The deceptive act of pretending to be another person, often by using false, altered, or stolen identification, with the intent to commit fraud.
- **Incarcerated Individuals:** Persons held in jails, prisons, or other correctional facilities, for whom notaries may perform services under specific protocols, requiring heightened vigilance.
- **Incomplete Documents:** Documents presented for notarization that contain significant blank spaces or missing information in critical areas. Notarizing such documents is a prohibited act.
- **Indemnification (Bond):** The legal right of the surety company (the bonding company) to seek full reimbursement from the notary (the "Principal" of the bond) for any funds that the surety company pays out to an injured member of the public due to the notary's error or misconduct.
- **Ink Color (Notary):** The specific color of ink (typically dark, permanent blue or black) that is required or recommended by state laws for a notary public's wet-ink signature and the impression of their official seal on paper documents.
- **Intentional Misconduct:** Deliberate and willful wrongdoing by a notary in their official capacity, often leading to criminal liability.
- **Interpretation (Document):** The act of explaining the meaning or legal effect of a document's clauses, terms, or phrases. This is a **prohibited act** for notaries (UPL).

J

- **Journal (Notary Journal):** A chronological, permanent, and often bound record book that a notary public is typically required by state law to maintain. It documents the details of every notarial act performed, serving as a critical audit trail and defense against claims.
- **Judgments (Civil):** Formal decisions by a court in a civil lawsuit, often ordering a party (e.g., a negligent notary) to pay monetary damages to another party.
- **Jurat:** A solemn notarial act in which a signer personally appears before a notary public, is identified by the notary, **signs a document in the notary's direct physical presence**, and then takes a verbal oath or affirmation, swearing to the truthfulness of the document's contents.

K

- **Knowledge-Based Authentication (KBA):** A sophisticated technological identity verification method primarily used in Remote Online Notarization (RON). KBA involves presenting a signer with a series of challenging personal questions generated from public and private data sources.

L

- **Last Line of Defense:** A metaphor describing the notary's critical position as the final opportunity to intercept a fraudulent transaction before it gains legal effect or causes widespread damage.
- **Legal Advice:** Professional counsel, interpretation, or guidance on legal matters, which notaries are strictly prohibited from providing unless they are also licensed attorneys. Providing legal advice constitutes the Unauthorized Practice of Law (UPL).
- **Legal Basis (Notary):** The specific laws, statutes, administrative rules, and regulations enacted by a state legislature or its authorized agencies that legally establish,

define, authorize, and govern the duties, powers, and limitations of a Notary Public.

- **Legal Clarity:** A clear and precise understanding of legal requirements and boundaries, essential for notaries to operate compliantly.
- **Legal Entanglements:** Involvement in complex and costly legal disputes or litigation.
- **Legal Framework (Notary):** The entire body of laws, regulations, and ethical principles that govern the Notary Public office.
- **Legal Presumption of Authenticity:** The legal principle that a document bearing a proper notarial certificate and the notary's official seal is presumed to be genuine and properly executed in a court of law, unless strong evidence proves otherwise.
- **Legal Responsibility:** The obligation to adhere to laws and regulations, and to be accountable for actions and omissions.
- **Legal Significance:** The profound legal weight, importance, and consequences of a notary's actions, impacting the validity and enforceability of documents.
- **Liability:** A broad legal term referring to an individual's or entity's legal responsibility for their actions or omissions, particularly when those actions or omissions cause harm, injury, or financial loss to another party. For notaries, liability can be civil, criminal, or administrative.
- **Limited Liability Company (LLC):** A business structure providing personal liability protection to its owners.
- **Loan Signing Agent (LSA):** A highly specialized Notary Public who has received additional, specific training and often certification to expertly guide borrowers through the signing and notarization of complex real estate loan documents.
- **Loans:** Financial transactions where money is lent, often secured by notarized documents.
- **Loss of Commission:** The temporary suspension or permanent revocation of a notary's commission by the state commissioning authority, ending their ability to practice.

M

- **Magnifying Glass:** A tool used by notaries to scrutinize tiny details, micro-printing, and security features on identification documents, aiding in the detection of forged or altered IDs.
- **Mandates (Legal):** Specific requirements or commands set forth by law or regulation that notaries must follow.
- **Medical Documents:** Legal papers related to an individual's healthcare decisions, medical treatment, or health records, often requiring notarization.
- **Meticulous Record Keeping:** The diligent, precise, and thorough practice of maintaining accurate, complete, and chronological records of all notarial acts performed, typically in a notary journal.
- **Micro-printing:** A sophisticated security feature embedded in many modern identification documents, consisting of extremely tiny text or patterns that are legible only under magnification.
- **Ministerial Role:** A crucial legal term defining the scope of a notary public's authority. A ministerial act involves following specific, prescribed procedures without exercising discretion or interpreting legal principles.
- **Misconduct (Notary):** Any improper, unlawful, unethical, or negligent behavior by a notary public in the performance of their official duties.
- **Misconception (Notary Bond):** The common misunderstanding that a notary bond protects the notary, when its purpose is actually to protect the public.
- **Mobile Notary:** A Notary Public who offers the convenience of traveling to a client's preferred location to perform notarial acts.
- **Moral Imperative:** A strong ethical obligation to act in a certain way (e.g., to protect the vulnerable), even if not explicitly mandated by law.
- **Mortgages:** Legal instruments used in real estate financing that pledge a property as collateral for a loan. Mortgages (or Deeds of Trust) are critical documents that almost always require notarization.

N

- **Negligence (Notary):** In a legal context, negligence refers to the failure by a notary public to exercise the degree of care that a reasonably prudent and competent notary would exercise in similar circumstances, resulting in harm or financial loss to another party.
- **Notarial Act:** An official, legally authorized act performed by a notary (e.g., Acknowledgment, Jurat).
- **Notarial Certificate:** The written statement, formally executed by the Notary Public, that attests to the specific facts of a notarial act. It is appended to or included within the document and serves as official, legally recognized evidence of the notarization.
- **Notario Fraud:** A specific type of fraud, often targeting immigrant communities, where an individual misrepresents themselves as having legal authority (like an attorney) to provide legal advice or services, which they are not licensed to do in the U.S.
- **Notarizing Incomplete Documents:** A prohibited act for notaries that involves notarizing a document that contains significant blank spaces or missing information in critical areas.
- **Notarizing Without Personal Appearance:** A fundamental and almost universally prohibited practice for traditional, in-person notarizations, where the notary performs an act without the signer being physically present. This is a direct gateway to fraud.
- **Notary Bond:** See **Bond (Notary Bond)**.
- **Notary Journal:** See **Journal (Notary Journal)**.
- **Notary Public:** An individual officially commissioned by a state government to serve the public as an impartial witness to the signing of important documents and to administer oaths and affirmations.
- **Notary Public Code of Professional Responsibility:** A widely recognized set of ethical guidelines for notary conduct.

- **Notary Seal:** The official stamp or embosser used by a notary public to authenticate their notarial acts on paper documents, containing specific information required by state law.

O

- **Oath:** A solemn, formal, and legally binding promise, often invoking a deity or a sacred entity, that a statement made is true.
- **Oath of Office (Notary):** A formal promise made by a new notary to faithfully and impartially discharge their duties according to state law.
- **Obligation (Legal/Ethical):** A duty or commitment that a notary is bound to fulfill by law or moral principles.
- **On-Demand Service:** Services available to clients when and where they need them, a hallmark of mobile notary work.
- **Operational Excellence:** A proactive and continuous commitment to the highest standards of practice in notary duties, characterized by unwavering precision, meticulous diligence, and continuous improvement.
- **Oversight (State):** The role of the state commissioning authority in monitoring, regulating, and enforcing compliance among Notaries Public.

P

- **Penalties (Legal):** The various legal consequences (e.g., fines, imprisonment, commission suspension/revocation) that a notary may face for violating notary laws, engaging in misconduct, or causing harm through negligence.
- **Perjury:** The criminal offense of knowingly making a false statement under oath or affirmation. Notaries administer oaths to deter perjury.
- **Personal Appearance:** The fundamental and non-negotiable requirement for almost all traditional, in-person notarial acts, mandating that the signer be physically present before the notary.

- **Personal Assets:** An individual's private property and financial holdings (e.g., home, savings) that can be at risk in a civil lawsuit if not protected by appropriate business structures or insurance.
- **Personal Financial Ruin:** A catastrophic financial situation where an individual loses most or all of their personal assets, often resulting from a large civil judgment.
- **Personal Safety:** The notary's paramount concern for their own security and well-being during appointments, especially when performing mobile notarizations.
- **Photo Substitution:** A fraudster tactic where the original photograph on a genuine identification document is carefully removed and replaced with the imposter's photograph.
- **Ploys (Psychological):** Manipulative tactics used by fraudsters to pressure, distract, charm, or intimidate notaries and signers.
- **Power of Attorney (POA):** A critical legal document that grants one person (the "Agent") the authority to act on behalf of another (the "Principal"). Notarizing a POA requires heightened vigilance due to its high fraud risk.
- **Precision (Notarial Acts):** The accuracy, exactness, and meticulous attention to detail required in performing all notarial duties, especially in completing certificates and making journal entries.
- **Presumption of Authenticity:** The legal principle that a document bearing a proper notarial certificate and the notary's official seal is presumed to be genuine and properly executed in a court of law.
- **Principal (Notary Bond):** The Notary Public (you) in a surety bond agreement, whose performance is being guaranteed.
- **Proactive Approach:** Taking initiative to anticipate and prevent problems, rather than merely reacting to them.
- **Professional Conduct:** The ethical and competent behavior expected of a notary public in all their interactions and duties.
- **Professional Liability Insurance:** See **Errors & Omissions (E&O) Insurance**.
- **Prohibited Acts:** Specific actions that a notary public is legally forbidden from performing according to their state's

notary laws and regulations. Engaging in prohibited acts can lead to severe consequences.

- **Property Deeds:** Legal documents used to transfer ownership of real estate.
- **Property Theft:** The illegal transfer or seizure of real estate (property) through fraudulent means, often involving forged documents and compromised notarizations.
- **Protecting the Public:** The fundamental purpose of the Notary Public office and notary bonds, ensuring citizens are safeguarded from fraud and negligence.
- **Psychological Manipulation:** Insidious tactics used by fraudsters to pressure, distract, charm, or intimidate notaries and signers into compromising the notarial act.
- **Public Officer (Notary):** The legal status of a Notary Public, indicating they hold a position of public trust and serve the public impartially.
- **Public Trust:** The confidence, reliance, and faith that the general public places in the integrity, impartiality, and competence of a notary public.

R

- **Real Estate Closings:** The final, pivotal stage of a property transaction where ownership is transferred and financial agreements are finalized.
- **Real-World Examples:** Actual or hypothetical scenarios illustrating notary duties, risks, and best practices.
- **Record Keeping:** The diligent practice of maintaining accurate, complete, and chronological records of all notarial acts.
- **Red Flags:** Warning signs, indicators, or unusual circumstances that suggest potential fraud, duress, lack of awareness, or other issues that might compromise the integrity or legality of a notarization.
- **Refusal (Notarization):** The notary public's right and, more importantly, their fundamental duty to decline to perform a notarial act when any legal or ethical requirement cannot be met, or when red flags cannot be resolved.

- **Regulations (State):** Detailed rules and guidelines issued by state agencies to implement and enforce notary laws.
- **Reimbursement (Bond):** The surety company's right to seek repayment from the notary for any funds paid out from the bond.
- **Remote Online Notarization (RON):** A modern method of performing a notarial act where the notary and signer are in different physical locations, communicating via secure audio-visual technology.
- **Reputational Damage:** The harm to a notary's professional standing and public perception due to misconduct, negligence, or involvement in fraud.
- **Requirements (State):** Specific mandates for notary commissioning, duties, and supplies in each state.
- **Residency Requirement (Notary):** The need for a notary applicant to be a legal resident of the commissioning state.
- **Risk Mitigation:** Strategies and practices aimed at reducing the likelihood or impact of potential risks and liabilities.
- **Risks (Notary):** The potential for harm, loss, or negative consequences arising from a notary's actions, errors, or omissions.
- **"Rush Job" (Psychological Tactic):** A fraudster tactic where an individual creates an intense and artificial sense of extreme urgency, pressuring the notary to rush through the notarization process.

S

- **Safeguards (Notary's):** Layers of security and verification measures employed by a notary (e.g., ID verification, journal, seal) to protect documents and prevent fraud.
- **Satisfactory Evidence (of Identity):** The acceptable forms of identification that assure the notary of a signer's identity.
- **Scrutiny (ID/Document):** Meticulous and careful examination of identification documents or notarized documents to detect fraud or errors.

- **Seal (Notary Seal):** The official stamp or embosser used by a notary public to authenticate their notarial acts on paper documents.
- **Security Features (ID):** Embedded elements in identification documents (e.g., holograms, micro-printing, UV features) designed to prevent counterfeiting.
- **Self-Proving Affidavit (Wills):** A separate affidavit attached to a will, signed under oath, that simplifies the probate process.
- **Signer Awareness:** The notary's crucial assessment that an individual signing a document possesses a sufficient understanding of the document and notarial act.
- **Signer Willingness:** The notary's critical assessment that an individual signing a document is doing so freely, voluntarily, and without any form of duress.
- **Signature Comparison:** The act of comparing the signer's signature on the document and in the journal to the signature on their identification document.
- **Sole Proprietorship:** The simplest business structure where the owner is personally liable for all business debts.
- **Solemn Act:** A notarial act that involves a formal verbal declaration (oath or affirmation), carrying higher legal gravity.
- **State Commissioning Authority:** See **Commissioning Authority**.
- **State Laws (Notary):** The unique statutes, rules, and regulations governing the Notary Public office within each individual U.S. state.
- **Statutes:** Laws enacted by a state legislature.
- **Subpoenas:** Legal orders compelling a notary to appear in court or produce records (e.g., their journal).
- **Surety (Bond):** The bonding company (financial institution) that issues a notary bond, guaranteeing the notary's performance up to the penal sum.
- **Sympathy (Psychological Tactic):** A fraudster tactic where an individual appeals to a notary's emotions by presenting a sob story or claiming dire circumstances, hoping to convince the notary to bend the rules.

T

- **Tampering (Document):** Unauthorized alteration or manipulation of a document's content.
- **Testator:** The individual who makes and signs a Last Will and Testament.
- **Threats (Duress):** Unlawful pressure or intimidation used to coerce a signer.
- **Thumbprint (Journal):** A mandatory entry in the notary journal in some states for specific document types, serving as an additional identity verification and fraud prevention measure.
- **Title Companies:** In real estate transactions, companies that conduct title searches, issue title insurance, and often act as escrow agents.
- **Training (Notary):** Formal education, instruction, or certification programs designed to equip notaries with the necessary knowledge and skills.
- **Trust (Public):** The confidence and reliance placed by the public in the integrity, impartiality, and competence of a notary public.
- **Types of Liability:** The various categories of legal responsibility notaries face: civil, criminal, and administrative.

U

- **Unauthorized Practice of Law (UPL):** A severe legal and ethical prohibition that prevents individuals who are not licensed attorneys from performing legal services. Notaries are strictly prohibited from UPL.
- **Unbiased (Notary):** The notary's neutral stance, free from prejudice or favoritism.
- **Undue Influence:** Improper use of power, authority, or a position of trust that deprives a person of their free will and substitutes another's objectives. Notaries have a critical duty to assess and guard against this.

- **Uniform Electronic Transactions Act (UETA):** A model state law adopted by most U.S. states that provides a legal framework for the validity of electronic records and signatures.
- **Unexpired IDs:** Identification documents that are still valid and have not passed their expiration date, required for notarization.
- **Unsuitable Environment:** A location for notarization that is too dark, noisy, public, or otherwise compromises the notary's ability to perform duties or ensure safety.
- **U.S. Citizenship and Immigration Services (USCIS):** Federal agency responsible for administering the nation's lawful immigration system, including oversight of the Form I-9.
- **UV Light (Ultraviolet Light):** A tool used by notaries to check ultraviolet security features on identification documents and currency, aiding in the detection of counterfeits.

V

- **Validity (Document):** The state of a document being legally binding, authentic, and enforceable.
- **Veneer of Legality:** The appearance of legitimacy that fraudsters seek to give to illicit documents through a seemingly proper notarization.
- **Venue (Notary Certificate):** The geographical location (state and county) where a notarial act physically takes place, a mandatory component of every notarial certificate.
- **Vigilance:** The state of being watchful, alert, and attentive to potential dangers, risks, or red flags. Unwavering vigilance is crucial for notaries to detect fraud.
- **Vital records:** Official government documents that record major life events (e.g., birth certificates, death certificates, marriage certificates). Notaries are generally prohibited from copy-certifying these.
- **Vulnerable Individuals:** Persons who may be susceptible to exploitation due to age, illness, language barriers, or lack of

legal understanding. Notaries have a moral imperative to protect them.

W

- **Willingness and Awareness:** Two critical elements a notary public must assess in every signer before performing a notarial act. "Willingness" means acting voluntarily; "Awareness" means understanding the document and act.
- **Wills:** See **Last Will and Testament (Will)**.
- **Witness (Document Witness):** An individual who observes a signer affix their signature to a document, often required by legal documents in addition to the notary.
- **Wrongdoing (Notary):** Any improper or illegal act committed by a notary in their official capacity.

About the Author: Derrick Spruill

Hello! I'm Derrick Spruill, and it's my privilege to guide you through the critical legal and ethical landscape of the notary profession. As a **highly respected Notary Public**, a **certified Loan Signing Agent (LSA)**, and the visionary **founder of Magnificent Workz Business Solutions, Mobile Notary by Derrick Spruill, and Notary Knowledge by Derrick Spruill**, I've meticulously built a career grounded in unwavering integrity, meticulous professionalism, and a profound commitment to public service—all illuminated by my deep faith. My journey into the notary profession began with a clear vision: to provide convenient, reliable, and expert notarization services that genuinely meet the demands of modern life, guided by a calling to serve.

My hands-on experience as a mobile notary has provided me with unparalleled, real-world insights into the operational intricacies of a notary practice. I've personally executed countless notarizations, from high-stakes real estate closings to critical estate planning documents, giving me a deep understanding of the precision required for certificates, journals, ink, and copy certification. This practical expertise forms the authentic foundation of my educational mission, driven by a desire to share the blessings of knowledge and empower you to operate without fear of legal pitfalls.

With an **MBA in Human Resources and a bachelor's degree in accounting from Walden University**, I seamlessly combine my robust educational background with **over 25 years of experience working for Fortune 100 companies**. This unique blend of academic rigor and extensive corporate experience provides me with invaluable insights into business operations, process optimization, and the critical role of meticulous compliance—all principles central to understanding and avoiding the liabilities discussed in this book. I passionately share this knowledge with my readers and clients, believing in excellence in all things, especially when it comes to legal adherence.

Beyond my direct client services and business acumen, I am deeply committed to community service and helping individuals in need, seeing this as an extension of my faith. I am a passionate educator and mentor, sharing my expertise to help others navigate the complexities of the notary profession. I am the creator of the acclaimed **"Notary Knowledge by Derrick Spruill" podcast**, where I share practical advice, critical ethical insights, and timely industry updates with a growing audience of aspiring and active notaries. My dedication to empowering others is further solidified through my comprehensive **"Notary Knowledge: The Complete Guide Series,"** a collection designed to elevate every notary's practice.

I firmly believe that a notary's role transcends merely applying a stamp; it is a **vital public trust** that demands continuous education, unwavering ethical vigilance, and an unyielding dedication to protecting the integrity of every document. My commitment to serving others is deeply rooted in the values instilled by my parents and the constant inspiration from my wife, who remains my greatest support. Above all, my life and work are guided by my love for my **Lord and Savior Jesus Christ**, believing that true service flows from a heart dedicated to higher principles. Looking ahead, I am also building on the fantastic world of Little Notary Derrick, aiming to bring notary knowledge to an even broader and younger audience, fostering an early understanding of integrity and civic duty grounded in timeless values.

In my free time, I enjoy expanding my knowledge by reading about business, following the thrilling world of NASCAR, and passionately cheering on my favorite NFL team, the Cincinnati Bengals. My wife and I reside in Herndon, Virginia, associated with World Changers Ministries.

Derrick Spruill's Core Values

My professional and personal life are guided by these foundational principles, illuminated by my faith:

- **Service First:** I believe the notary's highest calling is to serve the public with integrity, impartiality, and a genuine desire to assist, reflecting a spirit of selfless giving.
- **Knowledge is Power:** A notary's strongest defense against risk and fraud is a deep, continuously updated understanding of state law, best practices, and emerging industry trends, pursued with diligence and wisdom. This is especially true for legal and liability matters.
- **Professionalism is Non-Negotiable:** Every interaction, every document, and every client presents an opportunity to reinforce trust, build a stellar reputation, and exemplify the highest standards of the profession, honoring every task.
- **Embrace the Future:** Notaries must adapt to and master new technologies, such as Remote Online Notarization (RON) and Electronic Notarization (eNotary), to remain relevant, indispensable, and efficient in an increasingly digital world, recognizing innovation as a tool for greater reach and secure service delivery.
- **Integrity Above All:** Upholding ethical standards and maintaining unwavering honesty are paramount to the public trust placed in the notary office, rooted in a commitment to truth and righteousness.

Derrick Spruill's Goals

I am driven by a clear vision for the notary profession, inspired by my purpose:

- **Empower Notaries:** To equip every notary, from novice to veteran, with the comprehensive knowledge and practical skills needed to perform their duties flawlessly and confidently, fostering a community of excellence.

- **Elevate the Profession:** To raise the standards of notary practice across the industry, fostering a community of highly competent, ethical, and respected professionals, reflecting the high calling of public service.
- **Combat Fraud:** To serve as a leading voice and resource in the fight against document fraud and identity theft, protecting individuals and the integrity of critical transactions, standing as a shield for the vulnerable.
- **Promote Accessibility:** To ensure that essential notary services are accessible and convenient for all individuals, regardless of their location or physical limitations, through mobile and digital solutions, extending service to all who need it.
- **Inspire Future Notaries:** To ignite a passion for public service and legal integrity in the next generation, including through engaging content like "Little Notary Derrick," instilling values from a young age.

Books by Derrick Spruill

I am the author of the comprehensive "Notary Knowledge: Reference Guide & Notary Bible" and the following complementary books, designed to provide focused, in-depth exploration of key areas within the notary profession:

- **Notary Knowledge: Reference Guide & Notary Bible**
- **The Notary Public Foundation: Your Essential Guide to Core Duties, Ethics, and Commissioning**
- **Notary Operational Excellence: Mastering Certificates, Journals, Ink, and Copy Certification**
- **Notary Fraud Shield: Real-World Tactics, Red Flags, and Refusal Strategies**
- **The Mobile Notary Blueprint: Launching and Managing Your On-Demand Business**
- **Notary Niche Navigator: Your Guide to Loan Signings, Apostilles, I-9s, and More**
- **Notary Law & Liability: Understanding State Regulations, Insurance, and Avoiding UPL**

- **The Future Notary: Mastering RON, eNotary, and Complex Scenarios**
- **Quick & Easy Solutions: How to Increase Mobile Notary Business for More Success & Profit**
- **Learning with Derrick Activity Books** (Series)
- **Little Notary Derrick Children's Books** (Series)

End Notes for The Future Notary

As we conclude **"The Future Notary: Mastering RON, eNotary, and Complex Scenarios,"** and indeed, the entire **"Notary Knowledge: The Complete Guide Series,"** I want to express my profound gratitude for your dedication to expanding your notary expertise. My journey with Mobile Notary by Derrick Spruill and the "Notary Knowledge by Derrick Spruill" podcast has consistently reinforced the power of continuous learning and the incredible impact of our profession.

This series has been meticulously designed to guide you through every facet of notary work, from its foundational principles to the cutting-edge technologies of tomorrow. We've built your knowledge fortress brick by brick, empowering you to serve with unwavering confidence and integrity.

Remember these final, empowering takeaways that are the guiding stars for your lifelong journey as an exceptional Notary Public:

- **Your State Law is Your North Star:** Always consult your state's official notary handbook and statutes. This is your ultimate authority, ensuring every act is compliant and true.
- **Integrity is Your Ultimate Currency:** Your reputation for honesty, impartiality, and ethical conduct is your most valuable asset. Never compromise it.
- **Vigilance is Your Superpower:** Be a keen observer. Develop your ability to spot red flags against fraud, protecting both your business and the public.

- **Service is Your Calling:** Approach each client with empathy, professionalism, and a genuine desire to assist. Your service makes a profound difference.
- **Learning Never Stops:** Embrace continuous learning as a joyful pursuit. Stay updated on new laws, technologies (like RON and eNotary), and best practices.
- **Your Network is Your Strength:** Cultivate strong relationships with fellow notaries, legal professionals, and referral sources. Your network provides support, mentorship, and opportunities.

This series has provided a comprehensive foundation, but your journey doesn't end here. The world is constantly evolving, and so must your knowledge and skills.

Go forth with boundless confidence, with a joyful and open heart, and with the full knowledge that you are equipped for unparalleled excellence. The future of notarization is incredibly bright, filled with magnificent possibilities, and I can't wait to see the amazing things you will accomplish!

Thank you for allowing me to be your guide through this extraordinary series. It has been an honor and a privilege, and I look forward to witnessing your continued success.

— Derrick Spruill

www.ingramcontent.com/pod-product-compliance
Lightning Source LLC
Chambersburg PA
CBHW071353230926
51846CB00002B/533

* 9 7 8 1 9 6 5 8 9 6 2 9 7 *